"Ace has created a blue print that has been found tried and true thousands of times. You are fortunate that you don't have to reinvent the wheel or spend one more day struggling only to find another strategy that does not work. This is a play book for success in life in which Ace outlines a concise, consistent financial plan for Dentists that works."

—**Michael Abernathy,** DDS, Founder of Summit
　　Practice Solutions

"A superb book! Dr. Goerig demonstrates the keys to happiness and financial success. The core of his message is to become financially free while enjoying your life. Money in and of itself will not make you happy but having enough money to not worry about money allows you to develop your passions. Build enough wealth through conservative proven investments, get out of debt, gain perspective, and then use most of your time cultivating a life that is real, a life based on what you want, not what your parents or society tells you to be. Follow his advice, all of it, and I assure you that you will be 1,000% better for it!"

—**Alex Nottingham**, JD, MBA, Founder & CEO of
　　All-Star Dental Academy

"This book is one of the most comprehensive and compelling publications on the subject that I have experienced. It's uniqueness and what differentiates it from others is that it specifically addresses the lifelong needs and goals of dentists everywhere-issues and subject matter certainly not taught in our nation's dental schools. This book is a terrific read for all of us at any stage of our career, to and through retirement."

—**Hugh Habas**, DDS, New Jersey national presenter
　　on practice management

"All 'I've known Ace for 35 years and he has always been focused on value, quality, self-improvement, and mentoring others. This book is a continuation of those attributes and gives the reader the skills and knowledge to live a life of peace, joy, hope, contentment, achievement, and financial freedom. By putting his principles into action, you will be able to claim 'victory' and that success will spread to your office staff, your patients, and, most importantly, your family."

> —**James C. Kulild**, DDS, MS Past President, American Association of Endodontists, Diplomate, American Board of Endodontics, Professor Emeritus, Department of Endodontics UMKC School of Dentistry

"As a dentist in practice for 15 years I have often struggled with who to believe when it came to investing and a financial philosophy for life. I often was torn between what was the best way to live and spend and save. It is such an important topic with so many different opinions on the 'right way'. I found Ace 5 years ago and he and his philosophy have totally changed my life and all the secrets are contained in this short book. I truly believe that this is the "right" way and have made a commitment to read this book at the beginning of each year to remind myself. Thank you, Ace. I am now living a more meaningful, happy, purposeful, almost debt free life because of you and your relentless passion to help others."

> —**Derek White**, DDS, Madison, MS

"This book is one of the most comprehensive and compelling publications on the subject that I have experienced. It's uniqueness and what differentiates it from others is that it specifically addresses the lifelong needs and goals of dentists everywhere-issues and subject matter certainly not taught in our nation's dental schools. This book is a terrific read for all of us at any stage of our career, to and through retirement."

—**Hugh Habas,** DDS, New Jersey national presenter on practice management

"Here it is in a wonderful, compact nutshell—the 'crux' of the Ace Goerig philosophy of practice, personal finance, and life boiled down to this beautiful guide for happiness in our practice and personal life! Why 'recreate the wheel' when you have the best practice management mentor generously sharing his experiences and wisdom to us for a life filled with peace, joy and fulfillment? This book is a must-read for all dentists and gives us life skills to share with our loved ones, too!"

—**Richard C. Wittenauer**, DDS, diplomate, ABE, California

The Dentists 2019 Guide to Creating
Personal and Financial Freedom

by Dr. Albert "Ace" Goerig

Published by

ACG PRESS

222 Lilly Rd. NE
Olympia, WA 98506
DebtFreeDentist.com

THE DENTISTS
2019 GUIDE

TO CREATING PERSONAL
AND FINANCIAL
FREEDOM

DR. ALBERT "ACE" GOERIG

VIRGINIA BEACH
CAPE CHARLES

TABLE OF CONTENTS

PREFACE

AS DENTISTS WE HAVE one of the greatest professions and as Americans, we live in one of the greatest countries in the world with all the opportunities to have a life of our dreams. Many dentists have yet to find happiness and contentment in their practice and their lives. One problem is that we were not taught in dental school the secrets of creating a great, fun and profitable practice. Nor do we have enough education or understanding about personal finance and investing. We think we will get rich through investing, but many dentists lose money by placing it into several various so-called investments that they know nothing about, such as standard whole life insurance policies, risky stocks and speculative real estate, hedge funds, commodities, day trading, and limited partnerships, hoping they will strike it rich. We forget that the real money is made in our practice, and the best investment we can make is to pay off our debts first before we invest anywhere. Paying off debt is investing and gives you the maximum guaranteed return without any risk. We need to learn to love what we do and focus on creating a practice that is fun and profitable. My mentor, Kendrick Mercer, taught me that "Life is a process, not an end; if you don't enjoy the process, you'll hate the end!" This book is about learning to enjoy the process.

Through this simple and specific guide, you will be able to increase your practice profitability, pay off debts quickly and reach financial freedom while you savor and enjoy every precious moment of your life to the fullest. In this book, I will show you the most efficient way to become financially free by using the two vehicles that can get you an over 100 % return on your money, guaranteed. Using this approach, most doctors could be debt-free in three to five years and financially free in ten years. You will learn how to enjoy work more while creating an incredible relationship with your patients, team and family. The rewards are many. But most of all, I urge you to enjoy the process.

DR. ALBERT C. (ACE) GOERIG
Olympia, Washington
March 2019

FOREWORD

YOU ARE ABOUT TO make the most important decision of your life. This process will begin when you realize that your past does not define your future. You have the power to write a new personal and financial story. This journey begins when you delve into Ace Goerig's seven secrets for creating personal and financial freedom for dentists.

I have known Ace for decades as a friend. I've also followed his career as a super-successful endodontist and one of the best coaches I know. His newest book has the power to become *the* guide through the financial minefields of myths and mistakes where dentists find themselves during their careers. Make no mistake: waiting until you are in your fifties or later is exactly the wrong strategy for a safe, secure financial future. All of us should strive for a future with a variety of choices and options in our lives, which we can secure by the actions and decisions we make today. The scary part of this realization is that most doctors don't realize their mistakes until it is too late. When it comes to eliminating debt and saving money, starting as soon as possible is fundamental. As with most things in life, there is never going to be perfect timing or a perfect situation. The secret is just starting where you are, now. I have had the honor to speak to thousands of dentists every year, and the one thing that I find they share is a lack of understanding of the basics of debt and financial freedom. This misunderstanding or lack of knowledge is the fundamental element in every doctor's struggles. Learn to control consumption debt and you set in motion a life time of predictable wealth building.

For most of us, the struggle begins with the misunderstanding that debt is normal and unavoidable. Generations of people have assumed that they will always be in debt, and that it is OK. But nothing could be further from the truth. Ace will give you real-life examples of his staff members and friends who have bucked the trend and decided to re-write their stories. He has created a guide that has been found "tried and true," thousands of times. You are fortunate that you don't have to reinvent the wheel or spend one more day struggling, only to find another strategy that does not work. Ace outlines a concise, consistent financial plan for dentists, a playbook for success in life that works.

MICHAEL ABERNATHY, DDS
national speaker and founder of Summit Practice Solutions
Celina, Texas

After providing over 75 articles for *Dentaltown Magazine,* *Dental Economics, Dental Practice Report,* and *White Coat Investor* over the past decade, I count only a few precious authors who provide truly relevant and readable financial information for dentists. John Bogle, Warren Buffett, and Bert Malkiel have sold millions of books. I've now added Dr. Albert "Ace" Goerig to that list.

Ace's book, although a financial must for all dentists, shows us why a non-financial mindset is equally important. Ace provides the most efficient way to become financially free and enjoy every precious moment of your life. He gives us a step-by-step, easy, and frankly not painful, way to build your dream life with financial security. Ace has no hidden agenda. He's an old fart who's financially free, has a heart of gold, and is providing a living legacy with his work. Whether you are in dental school, a recent grad, in early to mid-practice years, or approaching retirement, Ace has your back. Overall, this 174-page gem is a must-read for all dentists of all ages.

DOUG CARLSEN, DDS

CHAPTER 1

Create an Incredible Life Story

IN A MAY 2017 INTERVIEW with Charlie Rose, Warren Buffett was asked what gave him his greatest joy. *"I love going to the office,"* said Buffett. *"It has been my painting for over fifty years: I get to paint what I want, and I own the brush and I own the canvas and the canvas is unlimited. And that is a pretty nice game, and I get to do it every day with people I like. I don't have to associate with anyone that causes my stomach to turn. If I were in politics, I'd have to smile at a lot of people I want to hit. I've got a really good deal and I am hanging onto it."*

Most dentist-owners forget that they have the brush and the canvas, and they can create their story any way they want. Sometimes it takes the insight of a coach to help them through the process.

CREATING YOUR NEW LIFE STORY

We are here on this planet for a relatively brief period, and all we have is from now until the end of our lives. So, how can we make the most of this time?

To live our lives to the fullest, we need to create a new vision or story of what is possible. We all can live the rest of our lives as a very exciting adventure. For most of us, because of our cultural context and the lack of training we have received regarding financial matters, it is difficult to set up a guide for reaching financial freedom, or even to recognize that our way of relating to money could be very different. However, if we write a story about how we want to live, it is easy to develop and follow a guide to fulfill that story. But most of us don't know how to develop a coherent and compelling story about financial and personal freedom.

I was raised poor by a single mom. I had a 2.3 GPA in high school and was only accepted into college because I set the state pole-vaulting record. I spent three years studying Engineering, and the Army ROTC taught me how to fly fixed-wing aircraft so I could fly helicopters in Vietnam in 1966. Instead, in 1965, I met my cousin who was a dentist, and he recommended that I go to dental school.

I changed majors and graduated from dental school six years later. I then spent twenty years in the Army as a Dental Corps officer. During that time, my family and I moved twelve times, had many different assignments, and really saw the world from a unique perspective. Life became an incredible story for me. The fun is in always developing new stories, so after I retired from the Army, I began a new story, and after a difficult start I created a very successful dental practice. Eventually I developed a dental consulting company to share my story with other dentists who were struggling, just as I had, so I could help them create a beautiful story for *their own practice and lives*.

The best stories are specific *and* flexible—specific in offering a full vision with rich detail, and flexible because life is a process and we are always growing. As new experiences arise, we begin to see things at a deeper level. When situations change, we need to give ourselves permission to change our minds to stay within our own integrity. You can create a beautiful story that incorporates abundance into your life. Having your finances in order will help support your positive story so you can live life fully. However, writing a life story takes great courage, because it involves change. Sometimes you need to change many things to live a free and independent life. In this case, you are called upon to face your fears of confrontation and conflict to create the life you want. Your story shows the world your intent to change and starts you on your new path. Gandhi was once asked, "What is your message to the world?" He replied, "My life is my message." What is your message to your children?

HOW TO BRING ABUNDANCE IN YOUR LIFE

The reason we create positive stories is to let the universe know what we want. I personally believe that we can bring anything—positive or negative—into our lives depending on our thoughts. This happens by creating a clear, positive vision of exactly what we want and know (believe) that it will come about. This could be an increase in referrals, doing more cases, finding the right associate or team member. Over 100 years ago, in his book, "The Science of Getting Rich," Wallace Wattles talked about focusing on what you want and not what you don't want in your life. We need to put our energies into the creative and not the competitive aspects of life. I never spend any time worrying about what the other dentist is doing. Why? Because there is unlimited abundance, if we have the right focus and vision, we can bring whatever we want into our lives. The real fun is helping others create abundance in their lives. I spend little time listening to the negative events in the news which I cannot control. The real joy and happiness comes from relationships with family and in my practice. Abundance always comes when we are thankful for all the gifts and richness that we have in our lives.

MY NINETY-YEAR-OLD MILLENNIAL STORY:
RETIRE IN PRACTICE

As members of the Baby Boomer generation, most of us were taught to work hard, put in the hours, take three weeks' vacation a year, and retire after forty years of practice to play golf and enjoy the sunsets. Yet many dentists still work after age sixty-five not because they *want to*, but because they *have to*, due to poor management of money, or because they have had too many "successful" marriages.

We look down upon the millennials because they seem to be more interested in enjoying life now, taking more time for themselves and their families, and are not as concerned with money as we Baby Boomers were. Yet down deep, those two generations are more alike than not. Because of our cultural imprinting, we did not know that we could write a better story. Both generations see the possibility. Let me tell you about my ninety-year-old millennial.

When I first came to Olympia, Washington as an endodontist in 1991, one of my favorite referring dentists came in for a root canal. He was in his seventies yet looked like he was in his forties. I commented on how great he looked, and I asked him what his secret was. He told me he had "retired in practice" only ten years out of dental school.

In the 1950s, when he had graduated, most dentists worked five days a week and took about two weeks' vacation a year. After a year in practice, his classmate told him that he could really work four days a week if he just modified his schedule, and he could make just as much money and have more time off. He did, and it worked. He told me he and his wife were not big spenders, so they were able to pay off the mortgage on their house and on the practice debt within ten years of graduation.

After that, he realized he only needed to work three days a week. He started taking more vacations each year to be with his family, enjoy his hobbies, take continuing education courses, and to relax and be much more creative in the way he ran the practice. He paid his team on salary, so they also had time off. He eventually retired at age eighty-two and enjoyed his very long and loving marriage. He came by my office in his early nineties and showed me pictures of himself skiing on the top of Mount Rainier with his great-grandson, and fly-fishing with his daughter. He recently passed away, shortly after his wife died. I am sure he enjoyed his millennial-style life.

What most of us do not realize is that we, too, can enjoy this retire-in-practice story (more specifics on how to retire in practice in Part Five). We just need to create it, and in dentistry we can. We can do this by getting out of debt as soon as possible, and by creating a practice that we love that is profitable and fun. Benjamin Franklin retired from business at age 46 to have more time to work on other interests and to contribute to the well-being of society while creating a personal legacy. What will be your legacy?

Don't do stupid things with money. The main mistake dentists make is living beyond their means right out of school and burying themselves in debt. Instead, know that you will have plenty of money to get out of debt quickly. Once you are debt-free, learn to invest consistently and safely on your own in a secure environment and you will never worry about money again. With the right guide this is all possible, and that is what I will show you in this book.

The Great American Scam consists of monthly debt payments, and has changed the American Dream into a nightmare. We are lulled into a false sense of security and ownership. The banks have trained (fooled) us to stay in debt our whole lives through credit cards, mortgages, refinancing and other loans, while they take from us two-thirds of our life's earnings in monthly debt payments. Unfortunately, most dentists do not understand how our money system really works.

A TALE OF TWO DENTISTS

Let's compare the tales of two twenty-five-year-old dentists.

Dentist A earns $200,000 a year. He has fallen for the scam and lives big. He buys the big practice, big home, expensive cars, and other toys to build ego and find happiness while continually creating debt and making monthly payments. He has no money for practice consultants.

After thirty years, he has paid off his mortgage, practice and school loan, but at age fifty-five, he still has a second mortgage, car payments, credit cards, timeshare payments and other debts, and only $225,000 in savings.

He resents going to work because he is working to pay off debt and not for the relationships or the fun of it. This creates poor relationships with his family, patients and team.

He will give to his creditors two-thirds of his life's earnings including the taxes he has paid on that income. Along with that, he will have given up his freedom and a life of choice which will keep him working for many more years because he *has to*—not because he *wants to*.

Dentist B also earns $200,000 a year. However, Dentist B lives simply, like a student, and she learns how to be profitable in dentistry, allowing her to pay off all debts, including credit cards, car, mortgage, school loans, and practice debt in ten years. She brings in a practice management consultant who helps her increase her net profit to $450,000 a year. Over the next few years she will increase her yearly net to over $700,000.

At age thirty-five, she has no debt, has retired in practice, and now works because she *wants to,* not because she *has to.* She loves going to the office three days a week with eight to twelve weeks off a year for vacation to be with her family and friends. She now has 60% to 70% of this income to invest for retirement, children's education, travel, or charitable contributions.

She has an associate, and the office is open five days a week. Even though she only works 120 days a year, she will earn more than Dentist A, except she will go to the office for the relationships and the fun, not because she needs the money. She now has the time to expand her relationships, enjoy other pursuits, and even make a difference in her community and the world. At age fifty-five, she will have been debt-free for twenty years and, because of her increase in net profit, her net worth is over $7,000,000.

You Can Become a Millionaire.

Here are the lessons from the book, *The Millionaire Next Door*, by Thomas Stanley and William Danko. Wealth is not the same as your income. Wealth is what you accumulate (net worth) and not what you spend. Wealth comes from hard work, dedication, planning and self-discipline. Millionaires do not live in upscale neighborhoods or drive fancy cars. A millionaire's goal is to become financially independent which is much more important than displaying high social status. These financially successful people control their consumption and do not allocate too much money to products and services. Millionaires are frugal and not only live below their means, they live *well* below their means. Most millionaires live in an average home, drive a used car and their children go to public schools. They are married to the same spouse who is also a conservative spender. Warren Buffett, one of the richest men in the world, has lived in the same modest house for more than sixty years, sent his children to public schools and drives an eight-year-old car.

We all have choices on where we want to spend our money.

We could buy a smaller house, go on fewer vacations, buy a smaller car or put more money in investments. Most people do not consciously sit down and consider their choices but instead they haphazardly spend their money without focus. Until we are debt-free, we are restrained by our income, so we need to create a game plan and focus our excess money to draw a guide of personal and financial success.

WRITING YOUR OWN STORY

Most dentists I work with want to have more time off to enjoy their family, hobbies and personal time. Many of them are burdened by long-term debt, are stressed at work and exhausted when they come home. They are unable to see the possibilities that life and their profession have to offer. Before they create the life, they want they must first imagine it. With the right vision and game plan, they could be debt-free within two to seven years, work three or four days a week in a drama-free, stress-free office with the people they like. Once debt-free, they could take six to ten weeks' vacation a year and have plenty of time to be with and create incredible relationships with family. So, whether you are a practice owner or an associate, you have the canvas and you have the brush to create the life of your dreams. This book was created for you, to show you the possibilities in your practice and personal life and give you the tools and ideas to create your story. As you go through the book, write down the things you want to change in your life, and the steps that you will take to create your new life story. The possibilities are endless.

CHAPTER 2

The Fastest Way to Become Financially Free

WHEN PUTTING ALL INVESTMENTS in perspective, the best returns are from paying off debt and increasing your practice profitability. These choices can give you a return of over 100%. Below are the past ten years' average returns on various investments.

- **Home**: 0-5%. According to Zillow, while home prices have appreciated nationally at an average annual rate between 3% and 5%, depending on the index used for the calculation, home value appreciation in different metro areas can appreciate at markedly different rates than the national average. Over time, home values grew about 0% after inflation. Plan on spending 5% of the value of the home to buy it, 10% to sell it, and 1% to 2% a year to maintain it.

- **Average actively managed fund investment**: 2.6%. According to *Forbes* ("Why The Average

Investor's Investment Return Is So Low," Sean Hanlon, Apr 24, 2014), the average investor in a blend of equities and fixed-income mutual funds has earned only a 2.6% or less net annualized rate of return for the ten-year period.

- **Inflation**: The current inflation rate reported by the US Department of Labor for the United States is 2.8% for the 12 months that ended May 2018. Remember that a 3% inflation reduces your 10% stock return to only 7%. But it also can reduce your 2% return on bonds to a negative 1%.

- **Short Term Bonds:** Over the past five years, bonds have returned only 1.4% annually.

- **S&P 500**: The most recent annual ten-year return on this index is 13%.

- **No fee investing**: Paying no fees on your investments results in **getting you up to 70% more on your investments.** Paying 1% to 4% in fees to financial advisors, brokers or mutual fund companies that actively manage your investments could cost you 70% of your return, making you work ten to fifteen years longer before you can retire. If you pay fees of 3% and your investments return only 4%, you got 25% of the return and your broker and mutual fund got 75% of the return. What happens when the return is only 2%? Your commissioned broker's mantra is "heads I win, tails you lose." Learn to invest on your own. This book will show you how.

- **Routine practice fee increases**: Can produce a 10% to 30% increase in net profit.

- **Paying off debt**: Up to 1000% (10x) return.

- **Dental practice management consulting**: Up to 1000% (10x) increase on return of investment over time.

Most of your advisors will not appreciate these numbers because each of them looks through a different lens based on their experience and training, and each of them will have a different agenda for you and your money. Your banker's motivation is to get your money into their bank, so they can loan it back to you. Your CPA gets paid to do your state and federal income tax and keep you out of tax difficulty. Because most accountants do not understand business and are risk-averse, their advice would be not to do coaching because they cannot understand the benefits and they see it as just an expense. Surprisingly, some CPAs are concerned that an increase in your net income would increase your taxes and that would be a bad thing. Your investment advisor will encourage you to put your money into your investments and a 401(k) plan, so they can continue to receive fees. When it comes to your money, you are the only one who cares more about it than any of your advisors.

You will see how the power of paying off debt can give you a guaranteed return of 100% to over 1000%, without risk or tax consequence. Many owner/dentists could significantly improve their net profit 100% in one year by bringing in a competent consultant. This is magnified to over 1000% in ten years.

Everyone needs to focus on what investment of your time and money produces the greatest returns. If you execute the last four strategies correctly, you will have more money than you will ever need, which you can trade in for time, freedom and choices. The market becomes a place to compound some of your excess money. I will show you the best strategies to safely get the best returns by yourself, without paying the extraordinarily high fees and commissions of financial advisors and brokers.

Once debt-free, a dentist would be able to maintain her/his lifestyle, fund their retirement and only need to work three days a week, and still take off eight to twelve weeks a year, which I call *retire-in-practice*. They could create a beautiful story and environment for themselves and their teams, and love going to the office knowing they have plenty of time off to play. Under those circumstances, why would you *ever* want to retire?

When this strategy is implemented correctly, you will have created an automatic investment program through index funds and you will not worry about the ups and downs of the market. Knowing that you are in for the long run and will not sell, eventually you can live off all the dividends of these funds. Remember that increasing the productivity of your practice and paying off all debt first, before investing in the market, will safely provide the highest returns with much more predictability.

FREEDOM FACTS

The fastest way to become financially free is to pay off all debts before you put money anywhere else. **The advantages to paying off debt first are:**

1. Easiest and simplest to do and understand.
2. Can make over 100% return on your money, guaranteed, without risk or tax consequence.
3. Can be done automatically, right out of your bank account.
4. Changes you from a spender into a saver.
5. You can now invest more into higher return stocks like the S&P 500 index fund because your paid-off home acts like a long-term inflation-adjusted bond. The 20% of your income that you were using to pay off your

mortgage now becomes a bond-like investment getting 20% return on your paid-off home.

6. Once debt-free, you have three times the amount of disposable income (previously, two thirds of your disposable income was paid toward debt) to spend on investments and enjoying life.

One of the biggest misconceptions that keeps you in debt that is perpetuated by banks and accountants is that you should not pay off your house early because when you have a mortgage, you can write off the interest rate on your taxes. This allows the banks to continue to get a large amount of interest from you using your money. If you are in the 28% federal income tax bracket, itemize your deductions and pay one dollar of mortgage interest and save $.28 in taxes. This means you lose $.72 of the one dollar to save $.28 taxes.

Let's look at this closely: in 2018 an average American couple who pays $10,000 a year in interest on their home loan has the choice of either taking the standard deduction of $24,000, or itemizing their return and taking the $10,000 tax write-off. When they itemize, they are unable to take the standard deduction of $24,000 and have an overall loss of $14,000 in standard deduction. The biggest loss is in the interest you paid the bank, which could range well over 200%.

Please consider a $310,000 mortgage at 4.5% for thirty years. Below, you can see that of the first year's loan payment of $18,849, only $5,001 goes to principal, but $13,848 goes to interest, which is lost forever to you. See Figure 1 below. *This is a 277% loan, not a 4.5% loan.*

In the 28% tax bracket, you had to earn around $17,724 and pay taxes on that to get the $13,847 to give to the bank as interest payments, which makes it a 354% loan. If you had paid an additional principal payment of $5,230.75, you would have eliminated one year's payment and saved $13,617.95 in interest and made 354% return on your money, guaranteed, without risk or any tax consequence.

Year	Interest	Principal	Balance
2019	$13,848	$5,001	$304,999
2020	$13,618	$5,231	$299,768
2021	$13,378	$5,471	$294,297
2022	$13,126	$5,722	$288,575
2023	$12,863	$5,985	$282,590
Total (after 5 years)	$68,833	$27,410	$282,590

FIGURE 1

The reality: over the next five years, you would have paid $96,243 in loan payments and only $27,410 would have gone to pay off the loan. You must understand that the interest is always the highest at the beginning of the loan, and for the first ten years of a 30-year loan the interest paid will always be more than 100%. Always take advantage of this guaranteed high return. **The bottom line: you invested $5001 and made $13,848, which is a guaranteed 277% return without risk. With this great return, why would anyone not use the money in their savings (only earning less than 1%) to pay off their home? You should also cash out any non-tax-deferred stocks and pay off debts.**

When we have debt, saving money is an encoded trap that keeps us poor. In the above example, if we have $100,000 in your savings or non-tax-deferred investments the best, safest and highest return on that money is to pay off debt. Paying $100,000 toward the $310,000 home mortgage would drop your mortgage to $210,000 and save you $121,360 in interest payments while paying off 13 years of the mortgage. Compare this $121,360 made by paying off debt to the $1,500 you would get with an after-tax return of 1.5% in a 2% bank CD on that same $100,000. You must see the $100,000 put into the house as a high return, safe long-term inflation adjusted bond that is always available to you through lines of credit or second mortgages. Once the home is paid off, the money used for mortgage payments becomes a constant source of available cash flow. It is like getting money from a bond.

Remember, focus on paying off debt before you put your money anywhere else. Once you are debt-free, I will show you specific investment strategies that provide safe and predictable results. Most people can be debt-free within five to ten years using this guide.

DEBT IS THE DEVIL

It's all about net worth. Our net worth is the total of all our assets, including our investments, bank accounts and real estate, minus our debts. Paying off debt increases your net worth (wealth) and provides an asset that you can use in emergencies as loan collateral. Paying off debt is a conservative investment strategy. So don't be happy about having more tax deductions, especially when you can't write them off due to the high standard deduction. This is how the government and the banks keep you in debt and in servitude.

There is no good debt; only bad debt. All debt is bad, bad, bad! Debt keeps you imprisoned and prevents you from living a life of freedom, independence and choice. Being overburdened with financial responsibilities increases your stress and can damage important and satisfying personal relationships and even lead to divorce which could cost half of what you own. By changing your spending and saving habits one step at a time, you can regain control of your life. You now know what interest payments really cost you and what to do to change your spending habits.

In John Cummuta's excellent audiobook and manual, *Transforming Debt into Wealth,* he states, "Every time you make a purchase on credit, you need to consider not just the price you're paying for the product, but the price plus interest plus how much that money could have earned you as an investment."

US households now owe $13.15 trillion in total debt, and about $931 billion of that is credit card debt, according to NerdWallet's 2017 American Household Credit Card Debt Study, along with its newly issued quarterly figures. In 2017, the average family's collective balance on all credit cards was more than $16,000. If the family makes just the minimum payment, it would take them thirty-seven and a half years to pay off the balance; over that time, they would make total payments of more than $43,000, of which $26,000 would be interest. This is just as if someone said to you, "I will lend you $16,000, and you will pay me back $43,000." If you were to invest the same $26,000 in an individual retirement account (IRA), it would grow to $284,329 over 30 years at 8% interest. We have spent tomorrow's money already and are making payments on it.

With each debt, the interest you pay puts you on the wrong side of the compound interest equation. It's important to realize that you are going to make a finite amount of money in your life. If you give too much of it away in interest payments and impulse buying, there will not be enough money left over for you to retire comfortably. You can take two basic approaches with your money: you can spend it on things that don't add meaning to your life and stay in debt and eat cat food in your retirement years, or you can build your financial future now by paying off debt early and retire early in style. Every dollar you consume now brings you one dollar of value, but every dollar you invest for your future can bring you five to twenty times that amount in your retirement years, allowing you to retire ten to twenty years earlier. Reducing spending and paying off debt will eliminate your money problems and improve your relationships. It will also improve your health by reducing stress. And it will serve as a shining example for your children about what is possible.

How would it feel to be out of debt and own your home free and clear, with utilities, taxes and food as your only real expenses? This is possible for everyone if they're following a clear guide. Most people can pay off all of their credit card debt in one year and their car in the second year. By the third year, they're making extra payments toward their mortgage. Most doctors can be totally debt-free within five to ten years and thereby eliminate payments on student loans, home loans and practice debts.

When you become debt-free, there is no need to worry about your credit report because you pay cash for all your purchases. *The ability to obtain credit is what got you into trouble in the first place.* The idea that you need to build up your credit by borrowing is an illusion that keeps you in debt. Once you become debt-free, no one owns you and this is true freedom.

HOW TO MAKE 1,000% INTEREST

Interest rates for dental school loans can average anywhere from 6% to 8% per year. Look at an actual 30-year, $300,000 dental school loan with an interest rate of 7.9% for which the doctor pays $2,180 per month. During the first year of repayment, only $2,556 goes to principal and $23,608 goes to interest. The doctor must earn around $30,000 and pay tax on those earnings, to cover that amount of interest each year. This is more than 1000% interest. **When determining how much student loan you will need, remember that for every $1000 you borrow, initially you will have to pay $10,000 in interest back to the bank which does nothing to pay back the loan.**

Year	Interest	Principal	Balance
2019	$23,609	$2,556	$297,444
2020	$23,399	$2,766	$294,678
2021	$23,173	$2,992	$291,686
2022	$22,928	$3,237	$288,449
2023	$22,662	$3,503	$284,946
Total (after 5 years)	$115,771	$15,054	$284,946

FIGURE 2

In this example, by making one additional principal payment of $2,766 that year, you will eliminate (save) $23,399 that you will never have to earn and give the bank, allowing you to make over 1000% return on your money. This is a no-brainer. Where else can you get 1000% return on your money, guaranteed, without risk? All those dentists who have student loans must focus on paying off this debt quickly— especially those who are paying high interest rates. If you paid an additional $3,888 per month, your payment would be $6,068 and you would pay the loan off in five years, thus saving $420,835, or about $550,000 before taxes. This is the best deal ever. **The reality:** If you decided not to pay off the loan in five years, then during that five years you would pay $130,825 in payments and only $15,054 would go to pay off the original loan amount.

STEPS TO GET RID OF YOUR DENTAL SCHOOL LOANS RAPIDLY

1. Just because they will give you a student loan does not mean you must take all of it. Remember, for every dollar you borrow you will initially have to pay back ten. Get a part-time job instead and borrow as little as you can handle.

2. Refinance your loan at a lower interest rate as soon as it becomes possible. Go to https://www.whitecoatinvestor.com/12-things-to-know-about-student-loan-refinancing/

3. Live like a student until all of your school loans are paid off. If you do not live like a student until your debt is paid off, you will most likely be living like a student when you are retired. This is the most important thing you can do in your career. Work as an associate for a few years. Take advantage of minority and veteran loans. Commit to paying your school loans off in five years. You and your spouse should create a game plan of getting out of debt which will give you freedom and choices and you can enjoy your relationship. Until you are debt-free, don't worry about getting expensive cars and homes that cause so much financial stress in relationships. Get a coach to show you how to increase your practice's net profit. Learn the secrets to greater efficiency and profitability in the next chapter.

STEPS TO ELIMINATE DEBT FOR THE
DOCTOR AND TEAM

Eliminating debt is a crucial first step in my guide. The only debt that is reasonable to incur is for the purchase of very large items such as your house, your education, your practice, or your car. Never go into debt for anything else, especially not for consumable items such as vacations.

I can't state it any more clearly: consumption debt is bad, bad, bad, and bad. The best guide is to spend less than you make and to save a substantial amount of your money. Then you can consume with saved dollars. Most families in America are imprinted to use their credit cards and consume, whether they have the money to pay for something or not. When you do this, you typically pay high interest rates; this is not an effective way to manage your money. Instead of a credit card, use a debit card. This way, you pay as you go and you eliminate interest payments. For a step-by-step approach to eliminating debt quickly, see Appendix B, Step-By-Step debt reduction plan.

CREATING A DEBT-FREE OFFICE

Early in my private practice career, I had a 401(k) plan and even a defined benefit plan. Because the plan was managed by financial advisors and brokers who invested into actively managed funds, the returns were dismal compared to the S&P 500 index fund. Most of my returns went to pay fees to my advisor and the mutual fund company. I also noticed that when people left my practice, they would immediately cash in their retirement plan and spend it on something stupid. If America's Best 401(k) plan had been available at that time, I would have moved my entire plan into that plan and maintained a retirement plan. But because the returns were so poor with my old plans, I decided to eliminate the retirement plans completely, and give each team member a $250 per month debt-reduction bonus. Even now, each year around the Christmas bonus time I have a dinner meeting with my entire team and their spouses, and show them how quickly they can be debt-free using the snowball approach as described in Appendix B. For other doctors who want to help their team get out of debt, I have included the entire audio and video program on my website: DoctorAce.com.

This has been in effect for more than six years, and I have four team members now completely debt-free, and most of my team are now paying off their homes. I have faith that they will be completely debt-free within six to ten years.

But my greatest gift to them is not being out of debt; my greatest gift is that I changed them from spenders into savers. This has done much to eliminate the money issues that many families argue about. Ironically, the only drawback to this plan is that three out of my four team members who are now out of debt do not need to work as much now, and they either work part-time in the practice, or they've left the practice to enjoy their hobbies, which can be profitable. I just bring more people in and get them out of debt. Here is an example of one of those team members.

LISA'S STORY

Lisa was my chief clinical dental assistant and was incredibly good at her job. She had a hobby selling things on eBay. Surprisingly, she was making over $50,000 a year in her hobby.

Her husband was making about $15 an hour on his physically demanding construction job. They decided to live on his income and focus everything she earned from their eBay business, plus her salary from my dental office, toward debt reduction and paying off their two houses. Within four years, they had paid off one mortgage and sold the other home and invested the profits into her company. Now debt-free, she and her husband both fund $5500 into their Roth IRA each year and put $15,000 into a self-employment SEP IRA. In 28 years, when they reach age 65, if they can get an average 10 % return on their Schwab S&P 500 index fund, they will have just over $2 million tax-free from the Roth IRA and an additional $2.3 million from their tax-deferred SEP IRA.

Lisa has since left my dental practice. She and her husband work about fifteen to twenty hours a week on their eBay business, and have plenty of time for travel and enjoying the adventures of life. They had their first child in November. It is surprising how, with strong intent, becoming debt-free happens very quickly.

HERE IS HOW TO ELIMINATE ALL OF A DENTIST DEBT IN THREE TO FIVE YEARS

Here is how to quickly pay off your dental debt. The average American dentist takes home around $200,000 a year. Most doctors live on $150,000, which gives them $50,000 per year to pay off debt. But the following chapters also describe how to become more *profitable* and/or use a dental practice management consultant to increase your income by $160,000 a year by just doing one additional large procedure per day, such as a crown. If your crown fee is $1,000 and you work 200 days a year, doing an additional crown every day would bring in $200,000 each year. After paying lab fees and materials on the $200,000, you will have made an extra $160,000 from the crowns. After paying taxes on the $160,000 you will still have an extra $120,000 each year to pay toward reducing debt. Add that to $50,000 of your original disposable income and you will have $170,000 to pay off debt. One more crown a day will give you an extra $14,166 each *month* to pay off debt. Once you are debt-free, you have that additional $14,166 plus your monthly payments of $10,127, equaling $24,293 per month ($291,596 per year) available for investing and your lifestyle. If this were invested in an S&P 500 fund returning 9% annually, you could have $16,370,956 in twenty years. This is called freedom.

$14,166 (1 Crown) Paid Toward Debt
Principal Each Month

Name of Debt	Total Balance (smallest to largest)	Monthly Payment	Accelerated Monthly Payment	Months to pay off
Visa card	$1,000	$30	$14,653	0
Master-Card	$1,500	$32		0
Car 1 at 6 % / 3 year	$14,200	$425		1
Car 2 at 6 % / 3 year	$21,300	$640	$15,293	2
Dental school at 6 % / 30 year	$300,000	$1,800	$17,093	18
Mortgage at 4.5 % / 30 year	$400,000	$2,000	$19,093	21
Practice at 4.5 % / 10 year	$500,000	$5,200	$24,293	21
Totals	$1,238,000	$10,127 ($121,524/ yr.)		63 months 5 yrs. 3 mo.

FIGURE 3

If you did *two* additional crowns per day, you would debt-free in 3 years and 9 months. In the Third Secret, there are ideas and systems that can double your net profit.

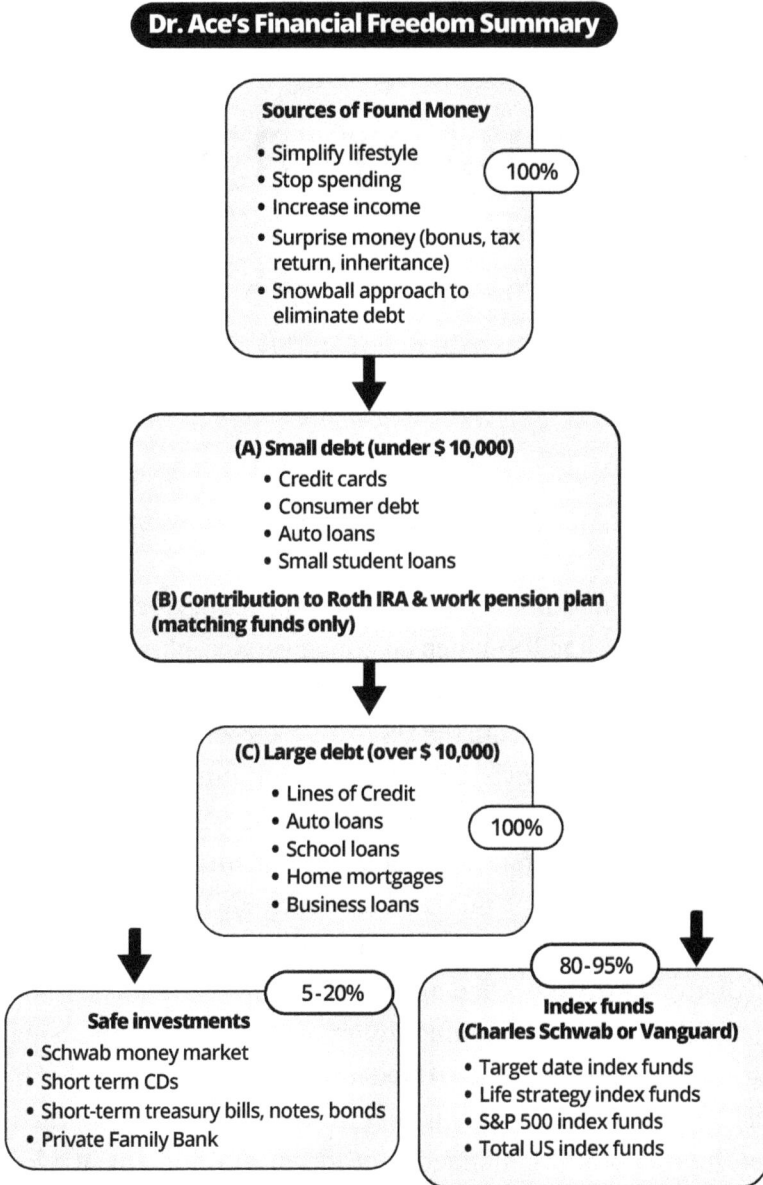

Dr. Ace's Financial Freedom Summary

Sources of Found Money

- Simplify lifestyle
- Stop spending   **100%**
- Increase income
- Surprise money (bonus, tax return, inheritance)
- Snowball approach to eliminate debt

(A) Small debt (under $ 10,000)

- Credit cards
- Consumer debt
- Auto loans
- Small student loans

(B) Contribution to Roth IRA & work pension plan (matching funds only)

(C) Large debt (over $ 10,000)

- Lines of Credit
- Auto loans   **100%**
- School loans
- Home mortgages
- Business loans

5-20%

Safe investments

- Schwab money market
- Short term CDs
- Short-term treasury bills, notes, bonds
- Private Family Bank

80-95%

Index funds (Charles Schwab or Vanguard)

- Target date index funds
- Life strategy index funds
- S&P 500 index funds
- Total US index funds

FIGURE 4

CHAPTER 3

Becoming More Profitable in Your Practice

YOUR PRACTICE IS YOUR economic engine, so optimize it to the fullest.

You can make more money in your practice by creating efficient systems, providing top-notch customer service, plus a loving and incredible team, high efficiency, and beautiful clinical results.

In 1991, I retired from the US Army after serving twenty years, including twelve moves and multiple job duties from general dentist, endodontist, endodontic resident mentor, and clinic chief, to commanding officer of a dental command. I was from the state of Washington, so when I retired, I just drove south from Seattle until I ran out of traffic and found the beautiful town of Olympia, which needed an endodontist.

A little afraid of opening my practice, I started in a small, three-operatory, 600-square-foot office that another dentist had just left. At that time, I knew very little about opening a practice and had no practice management ideas, so I brought in a local dental consultant to help me set up my systems. She was very helpful, and we implemented systems and hired three assistants and one office administrator.

Being one of only three endodontists for a population area of 200,000, I was swamped with patients and I was working five days a week, ten- to twelve-hour days, killing myself and my team. What I did not understand was how to schedule patients properly which resulted in excessive stress and very low production.

After the first year, I was exhausted and wondered if I should have just retired from dentistry completely. There was a lot of complaining and drama from my overworked team. Some days I would drive up to the office and think that I should maybe just keep on driving. One Sunday, I came into the office and was going through the front desk drawers and noticed a lot of bills that had not been paid, and checks that had not been deposited. It turned out that the woman up front was overwhelmed with her duties but had not told me.

Eventually, I realized I was nine months behind in payroll taxes, my life insurance had been canceled, and I was $250,000 in accounts receivable over 120 days because *I* did not know we needed to collect at the time of service, and *she* did not know we needed to send out statements. We were basically living on insurance payments.

Because I had lectured nationally, I knew most of the great practice management coaches on the circuit, and the best coach I knew was Linda Miles. I hired her to come in and turn my practice around. She was incredible, and taught me the importance of real systems, such as scheduling, marketing, and creating a superior team.

I also learned how to use practice monitors and know the numbers I needed to track, including understanding my profit and loss (P&L) statement. I hired a local bookkeeper to teach me how to use QuickBooks. I did my own QuickBooks for six months to better understand my overhead expenses and learn the ins and outs of QuickBooks. Then I hired the same local bookkeeper to come to my home office twice a month and enter all of my personal and business numbers from my checkbook and credit card statements into QuickBooks. He also balances my checkbook and prints out all checks, including refunds. Each quarter he does my 941 federal tax return, state unemployment and state disability taxes and city taxes. I also had him set up QuickBooks $500-a-year payroll accounting program. This saved me from working with a payroll service at $2000 a year, and it was much easier for my office manager to put in payroll hours. I pay my bookkeeper $36 an hour and last year paid him $1,900 for my business and $600 for my personal accounting. He has a great knowledge of taxes and works very closely with my CPA. I have an excellent CPA who oversees everything, gives me advice, and does my tax returns for around $7,000 per year. She is very responsive, up to date, thorough and understands the IRS codes and makes me follow the rules.

I review the profit and loss statement and office production monitors monthly. You need to have good practice monitors which you can obtain from one of your fellow dentists or a dental management coach. When you understand and monitor the numbers, there is less chance of embezzlement (staff-initiated bonus), an unfortunate but always real possibility. A two-doctor general dentistry practice in my town was embezzled for $1.9 million over seven years, and it can happen to you if you don't know your numbers.

We hired new employees and an experienced administrative team member. I reduced the number of patients I saw, focused on enjoying each individual patient and the dentistry, and even got home on time. Within a month, I was much more profitable, doing procedures I loved.

Since that time, I've had many different practice management consultants come into my office, and every time it has been of great value. I have always had an interest in the business of dentistry and will share with you what I have learned from these consultants. I have been fortunate to be in one of the best dental communities in the country where dentists are open to sharing and helping other new dentists in our community. Many of the ideas that I'm sharing with you come from my dental consultants, and from the dentists in my local community and from what I have observed in their practices.

The annual collections for the average dental office in the United States is around $700,000 with an overhead of around 69%, resulting in a net of $220,000 for the doctor. In this chapter you will find many strategies to increase profitability and reduce your time in the office. Below are four successful practice models of some of the best general practitioners I know. Note that the doctor has empowered the team to run the office, which allows the doctor to have 98% of his or her time to focus on direct patient care. The office has a minimum number of employees to reach high production goals. Each of these offices used a practice consultant to improve efficiency and double profitability. With increased profitability, it does not take a practice long to become debt-free, thus resulting in personal freedom and many more life choices.

SUCCESSFUL PRACTICE MODELS

Dr. K. Classic 2/2/2 model. This is a mature dental practice with two administrative staff, two dental assistants and two hygienists. They all work four 8-hour days (32 hours) per week (185 days a year) with six weeks of vacation. The doctor is very efficient, highly skilled and a great communicator with his patients. He focuses on high quality restorative treatment and refers most of his periodontics, endo and oral surgery out to local specialists which further increases his efficiency. The team provides superior service to their patients and understands how to create an emotional connection with each patient. Dr. K collects $1.4 million per year with a 50% overhead resulting in a $700,000 net profit. Remember that 80% above your base overhead is net profit.

Dr. M. 2/2/2/1 model. This is an owner/doctor in her forties with one associate. There are two administrative staff, three dental assistants and two hygienists. The team works four eight-hour days (thirty-two hours) per week. The owner/doctor works three days a week (125 days per year) and the associate works two days a week (ninety days per year) compared to the average dentist who works 195 days per year. The doctor is very efficient, highly skilled and a great communicator with her patients. The practice has an excellent team that leads and manages the associate. They collect $1.9 million per year with a 68% overhead, resulting in a $600,000 net profit for the owner/doctor. This is also a retire-in-practice model.

Dr. H. 1/1/1 model. This model includes Dr. H. plus one administrative member, one assistant and one hygienist. They work four ten-hour days (forty hours) per week (180 days a year) with six weeks of vacation. The doctor is efficient, highly skilled, communicates well with patients, and has an excellent team. He collects $1.2 million per year with a 50% overhead, resulting in a $600,000 net profit. He believes that the extra eight hours per week (of which 80% is net profit) significantly increases his bottom line as compared to most offices that only work thirty-two hours.

Dr. R. (retired in practice) 1/1/1 model. Dr. R.'s practice includes one administrative member, one assistant and one hygienist. They all work three 9-hour days (twenty-seven hours) per week (125 days a year) and all take ten to twelve weeks of vacation. The team is paid on salary. The doctor is very skilled in dentistry and communication, and is efficient, with an excellent team. He collects $700,000 per year with a 50%

overhead, resulting in a $350,000 net profit. He has been debt-free for years and has a strong base of patients who continually refer new patients to him.

Each of the above dentists got out of debt quickly and invested in index funds as described in this book. Each became financially free in their early fifties.

CREATING THE OFFICE CULTURE

The action of writing your vision is the most powerful way to make your new story happen. Once written and shared with the team, it becomes the culture of the practice. When writing about your new vision, think about the movie *Jerry McGuire* and check out the YouTube video "Jerry Maguire Mission Statement."

Write a vision statement describing how you want your practice to be. This process will start you thinking about what is important to you in your practice as you create your office culture. A vision shows the world your intent to change and starts you on your new path. A vision makes a strong statement to the world about who you are and where you are going. It is like a magnet that will bring into your life all the ideas, people, and tools you need to make it happen. It is also like a compass on a ship: it allows the captain to sail in a specific direction and helps guide the changes he needs to make to get to his new destination. Below is my own office vision statement, which I placed at the front office where all patients can see.

> **My Office Vision:** We are in a continual process of creating a story for our practice that is both fun and exciting and brings each of us personal fulfillment, joy, peace, and freedom. Through dedicated people, ideas, and the use of systems, we will develop a positive, nurturing, and safe

environment to grow and fulfill our needs both personally and professionally. It will be a place of mutual respect, laughter, clear communication, and teamwork in an atmosphere that is fun, energized, and joyous. We will connect with our patients on a personal level and provide a patient *"Wow"* experience that it is so incredible that they will hesitate to leave our office for fear of entering a harsher world. Our office will have a reputation of high-quality treatment, being so gentle, safe, and caring that we will receive many new referrals from our existing patients. We will enjoy every day to the fullest and live in each moment. Our office will be filled with laughter, pride, a sense of ease, and a calmness that allows us to provide to each patient an experience that is unsurpassed.

CREATING AN EFFICIENT OFFICE

Most dentists waste two to four hours a day in unproductive procedures that take too long and do not even pay the overhead. Many spend too much time on a poorly designed schedule doing small-case, average procedures. Too much time is lost on the phone or computer, on team management issues, or just talking too much. Many doctors think that improving their techniques, or getting new equipment, will increase their net profit, but the real profitability is in efficient office systems and training the team to run those systems. Dentists must learn to do dentistry and empower the team to manage the practice, so the doctor can stop spending extra hours on practice management. If you empower your team to run your practice, you only need three to four hours per month for practice management.

Many dentists try to coach themselves and go to practice

management seminars and then come back and try to train the team to change their systems. The problem is, they don't know which systems to change. That's why it is essential to have an on-site consultant observe office flow and the quality of the team members, and then evaluate which systems can be improved and which systems need to be changed. The dentist/owner needs to let go of any members of the team who cause unnecessary drama and frustration to the doctor and other team members. When the systems really flow well, patients love being in the office, the team loves serving the patients, and the dentist loves doing the dentistry. This whole process can be a lot of fun for everyone.

IDEAS AND SYSTEMS THAT CAN DOUBLE YOUR NET PROFIT

- **Phone and scheduling skills.** Today, most dentists feel they just don't have enough patient flow and believe they need to spend more time on external marketing. They could easily double their patient flow using effective phone skills with new patients. One of the best companies to help train your team on customer service and phone skills is All-Star Dental Academy. (https://www.allstardentalacademy. com/). Not only does All-Star have outstanding training programs that ensure new patients come in for an appointment; it also teaches your team superior customer service. The scheduling module is excellent, and All-Star now has a program on how to present (sell) the dentistry, all for just a few hundred per month.

- **Presenting and selling dentistry.** You have the greatest case acceptance when you have a doctor, team, and culture that can create an emotional connection with the patient. Because most dentists are uncomfortable presenting treatment plans and fees, this is best done through well-trained and incentivized hygienists.

- **Increasing internal referrals.** If you are not growing, you are not doing everything to inspire your patients to refer. Low intensity referral is from zero to twelve new patients per month. When you get below ten new patients per month, it probably means you are offending them. When you get thirteen to twenty-five, that is normal. Twenty-six to forty is good, and above that is excellent. If you're getting forty new patients a month and you are not growing, the problem is not consumerism, but capacity, which is space, equipment, staff, and doctor's speed. It only takes one of these factors to be substandard to bring the practice to a halt. With high referral intensity of twenty-five to forty new patients a month, patients are initiating the referrals. These are patients who call their friends just to tell them how incredible their dental visit was. When you obtain this level of referral intensity, you will draw patients from your entire area. Remember that 80% of your profitability comes from 20% of your patients. These are the patients that pay on time, appreciate you and your team, sing your praises and have friends just like them. Focus your internal marketing on those patients.

- **How do you achieve true referral intensity?** Patients love to find great value and share that with friends. If your patients get what they expect, then you're in the middle zone. If they get more than they expect, then you move to the highest level of referral intensity. Go through the office and rate each step of the patient experience as low, average, or high. Any phone calls must be gracious and encouraging. When patients come to the office, they should be greeted by the person they talked with on the phone.

Referral negotiation is best facilitated by the team rather than by the doctor, and the following script must be delivered exactly (note that it is important to employ pauses long enough for the patient to focus on what you're saying).

Before treatment: *Mrs. Jones, can I ask a favor?* (Pause) *If we can really impress you with how you're treated today, would you do something for us?* (Pause; wait for the answer. Once they agree, continue.) *If we can really impress you with how you're treated today, would you send us your friends, your family, and the people you work with?* (Then wait for them to respond.)

After treatment: *How did we do? Were you impressed?* (When they say "yes," give them a couple of cards with some type of discount or offer printed on the back, so they can distribute them to their friends.)

- **Creating an emotional connection with the patient.** This begins with your first phone call with the patient, which is more about listening than talking. Each team member and the doctor need to be trained to ask more questions about the patient and talk less about themselves, so we listen and talk with the patient focus coming from your heart.

Sometimes, we get very fearful of patients because of their poor past dental experiences. Before I meet the patient, my assistant tells me that the patient is very nervous, so when I come into the room and introduce myself, I tell them that I am very gentle. I will sit face-to-face with them and address their fears. I remind them that those fears from the past are embedded in their subconscious so they have no control of the fear when they come into the office. I also tell them that it takes great courage to face their fears and show up. Because of their courage, I promise them three things: I will always get them completely numb, they will always be in control, and I am very fast and efficient in my treatment delivery. This helps put the patient immediately at ease. Then getting to know the patient is fun. Here is a thank-you note from one of my patients that demonstrates the importance of emotional connection.

Dear Dr. Goerig, two weeks ago I got a diagnosis of breast cancer stage IV. Two days after that I woke up with a swollen cheek and learned I needed a root canal and ended up in your chair. I was still emotionally reeling from my health news but noticed the poster from your time at Fort Knox, Kentucky. I was stationed there as an Army dietitian and, when I shared all my story, you were so gracious, compassionate, and funny that you helped me relax and almost enjoy my time in your chair. Thank you for letting God use you to minister to me and reassure me of his love and care. You may not have been aware of it, but you were my angel that day! I still tear up thinking about it, how you verbally encouraged me, loved me and encouraged me further and then even reduced my charges, so I would not be facing such a huge bill. You are an angel and I can't thank you enough for being the conduit of God's love to me that day. I really needed it and won't ever forget it. God bless you and your whole family. With gratitude.

- **Same-day service.** There is another practice hidden within your practice. If you have a practice that schedules $75,000 per month, there is another $75,000 hiding in same-day service. The hygienist reminds patients of a condition that has already been diagnosed or just found and asks them if they would like to do the treatment that day. Case acceptance is far higher with same-day service. Once your office embraces the idea of same-day service as a normal part of doing treatment, handling the finances is not a problem. We only incentivize same-day service that is highly productive ($700 or higher) and that we want to do. The bonus for the person who gets a patient to say "yes" is $10, and the bonus for the assistant is $5. Same-day service is the secret to a high case average. When you try to sell harder on the first appointment, you can drive patients away from your practice. When case average (total practice production divided by all new patients) rises above $2,500, referrals go down. When case average rises due to same-day service, referrals may rise at the same time. Low case average usually means high volume, which means more staff, more overhead and lower profitability.

- **Bonus system.** When I was in the Army for twenty years, I would work very hard for three years in an assignment to get a $0.10 ribbon. This same incentive doesn't work as well in civilian life, but showing your appreciation through bonuses and thanking them often *does* pay big dividends. One of the most effective ways to increase profitability is to implement a smart and effective bonus system that can motivate your team while it increases your net profit. To make a bonus effective, everyone on the team must understand how the bonus is calculated. It is much better to give bonuses on a daily or monthly basis instead of yearly. That way, you get much more excitement and participation from the team. Bonuses should be designed to reward the entire team, not just individuals, although individuals can be rewarded for making same-day service work or for increasing case acceptance.

- All bonuses must be based on collections, with the understanding that total team compensation should not exceed 20%. Large purchases should not be added to average overhead expenses when considering this 20%. When you are trying to help your team get out of debt, remind them that bonuses can accelerate their debt reduction. There are many types of bonus systems out there and I would highly recommend that you work with a practice consultant who will help you implement a bonus structure that works best for you in your practice. I feel the best and most immediate bonus that you can give your team is to compliment them and thank them often for specific things, such as filling the schedule properly, creating great relationships with your patients, and making same-day service work. Individually, I thank each of my team players for being part of our incredible team.

- **Adult oral sedation dentistry:** Fear of dentistry is one of the main reasons that only 65% of the population go to a dentist. Many of those with the greatest fears have extensive dental work that needs to be done. Becoming certified in adult oral sedation will help you take better care of your fearful patients and is available for those patients who would like to have extensive work done all at one time under sedation. The best course for dentists is provided by DOCS education. It is by far one of the best courses I have ever taken. They also have an IV sedation certification course. https://www.docseducation.com 855-227-6505

- **Practice membership.** In this model, the patient pays a certain amount each year such $150 to $197 per person, which includes a 10% to 15% discount on all the dentistry during the membership year. For this membership, you provide an exam, x-rays and two cleanings per year (you can knock off $20 for children). You can offer to upgrade patients to this program once they need dental treatment. Membership patients are usually uninsured but can be offered discounts to encourage large treatment plans. Some states are trying to restrict practice membership plans due to the pressures of dental insurance companies; check with your state. One of the best sources to help you in creating the practice membership program is Ben at veritasdentalresources.com.

- **Focus on the dentistry that is less stressful and more profitable**. Focus on and become extremely efficient on the 20% of the dentistry that gives you 80 % of your profit. It always seems that the most profitable and successful dentists in town refer out a lot of their specialty work. The average profitable dentist in our area collects around $800,000 and takes home only $300,000 net. One of my best referrals learned from the prosthodontist how to use very sharp diamonds to do incredible, beautiful crown preparations in five to ten minutes. This doctor collects about $1.5 million per year and takes home around $750,000 net. This is because he focuses on the things he does efficiently and less stressfully and refers out the rest. The reason for the high net is that most of the collections above $800,000 go to net profit. He once told me that the greatest enemies of the general dentist are difficult patients, stressful procedures and unpredictability. That is why he refers most of his endodontics and other nonrestorative treatments out to specialists. I have personally found that the most profitable dentists in my community have strong professional relationships with the specialists.

DEVELOP A WIN-WIN RELATIONSHIP WITH YOUR SPECIALIST

- Specialists help you to be more profitable by allowing you to refer those cases that are stressful and not profitable, instead to focus on the dentistry you do best. They are a resource for you to expand your knowledge and can help and support you with difficulties in treatment. They are a second opinion and support your treatment plan. I also like to tell referred patients what a great office and dentist they are coming from during my treatments. Specialists also can be a source of referrals. And one thing that is often overlooked is, the more we share, the more abundance comes into our lives.

IDEAS ON HOW TO IMPROVE SPEED AND QUALITY

- **During the day, have your dental assistants time you.** If you are taking too long on various procedures, such as molar root canals, get additional training or refer out to a specialist. Ask your local supply rep for the name of the best and most respected dentist in town and ask the local lab owner which dentist does the most crown work with the highest quality. Call the doctor and ask if you can observe them in their office. You may want to video the procedure. Ask if you can bring your chief clinical assistant and front-office team member to observe the flow of the practice. Buy lunch for the doctor's team. Meet with the doctor for dinner and ask if he or she will mentor you. All great dentists are always looking for someone they can teach. Get involved in local study clubs.

- **Add new profitable services to your practice** and learn to master them. Such services may include Invisalign or dental sleep medicine that focuses on the use of oral appliance therapy to treat sleep-disordered breathing, including snoring and obstructive sleep apnea (OSA).

- **Buy the patients from another practice** when that dentist is retiring.

- **The office should be a place of safety and peace for the entire team.** Fire all employees who create drama in your practice. You cannot change people, but you can change people.

- **Handling clinical or office frustrations.** When things are not going exactly the way you want, don't get upset, just laugh. Or you can use the following words to refocus and stay on task: *great, next, isn't that interesting,* or *it is what it is.* Frustration and anger are detrimental in obtaining high quality clinical results and creating a fun and profitable office.

- **An updated, superior website.** This is one of the first places a referred patient will go to check you out. It must have good photos, good information and testimonials from your patients. It should be designed so that your website on your phone looks exactly like it does on the computer. It should have a patient review area and a testimonial section. It is a good idea to have these testimonials moving across the page so when a patient looks at their phone, they see the testimonials. One of the best web design companies for dentists is PBHS.com.

- **Addressing negative family and cultural imprints about success.** Many dentists do stupid things with money because they have no formal training in understanding financial matters. But the biggest issues are the imprints and cultural beliefs about money that we learned from our family. Some examples are: you have to work hard to earn money; getting rich is a matter of luck; money is the root of all evil; when things are going good, they will always go bad. You may have felt unworthy as a child, and this imprint prevents you from being successful and profitable in your practice, thus causing you to sabotage your own success in practice and your investments. One of the hardest things I need to do, as a coach, is to help clients get past their low deserve level that is embedded in their subconscious and prevents them from becoming more profitable and happier in their lives. This is also true when investing their money. The purpose of this book is to provide a simplified investment game plan that keeps my clients away from financial advisors, risky investments and other situations where they would lose their money. I knew one doctor who continued to self-sabotage in his investments and practice. He fortunately got a great dental coach who helped him create a highly profitable practice, and he was finally able to put enough money away so he could retire. After he sold his practice and retired, he had all the money he needed to enjoy a fun and exciting retirement. Unfortunately his inner demons took over again, and he invested all his earnings from the practice into a real estate deal where he lost it all. For those doctors who continually self-sabotage and do stupid things with money: you may find yourself living on your Social Security in your children's home and taking vacations in a 200-mile radius.

If you have poverty consciousness imprinting or a low deserve level, you need to get professional help to break your behavioral patterns around money. One company that has helped many of my coaching clients is Legacy Life Consulting at https://www. legacylifeconsulting.com/. They will help you address the issues that cause you these problems and help you understand prosperity consciousness. With their help, you can create a story that allows you to expand your life and move out of your old comfort zone.

- **Become a stronger leader.** The owner/doctor is the source and responsible for writing the vision based on his or her core values, which create the culture of the practice. Leaders must be authentic and trust in themselves, always learning and open to all possibilities and willing to accept change. When you are not leading and paying attention, there will be much more drama in the team because they have lost respect for you. Great leaders empower their team to lead, but each senior team member knows the vision and direction of the practice is coming from the doctor. Doctors will sometimes give up the leadership role because they're trying to be the nice guy and they do not like conflict. But when the doctor gives up the leadership role, someone will step in to take over that role. When you get clear and want to step back into the leadership role, you will get push-back by the person who has led the team, and they will resent you because it appears you did not appreciate their efforts. This may end up in the dismissal of that great employee. Great leaders win hearts before minds. Read Simon Sinek's book, *Start with Why: How Great Leaders Inspire Everyone to Take Action*. Here are a few ways to keep growing as a leader:

- ☐ Give up control, delegate, and empower the team.
- ☐ Get out of the way, but follow up.
- ☐ Know the numbers (use practice monitors).
- ☐ Spend 98% of your time in direct patient care.
- ☐ Lead by example and be the best employee.
- ☐ Tell the team what you want.

- **Small practice changes result in enormous increases in net profit**. It is amazing how an increase of just one more crown a day (by doing same-day service) can affect your net profitability. Look at the chart below. One more crown per day increased the net profit by 181%, from $197,647 to $357,647, resulting in a net annual income increase of $160,000. If you did two additional crowns per day, you would realize an extra $320,000 in increased net income. With this extra $320,000 per year, your entire school loan debt, home, and practice loan could be paid off in five to six years. Once you are debt-free, you will have three times the amount of money to be able to work less, invest, and enjoy your personal freedom. This is all possible if you are open to new ideas and dental coaching.

	One More Crown per day		Average Dentists	
	Amount	%	Amount	%
Collections	$802,583	100%	$602,583	100%
Overhead	$444,935	39%	$404,935	67.2%
Net profit	$357,648	61%	$197,647	32.8%
Daily collections	$4,013/day		$3,012/day	
Monthly collections	$66,881/month		$50,215/month	
4 days/ week worked	200 days/year with two weeks off			

FIGURE 5

Here are a few great websites for practice management ideas. Each of these also offers practice management coaching.

https://blatchford.com/category/podcast/
https://summitpracticesolutions.com/
https://www.whitehallmgt.com/
https://growingyourdentalbusiness.com/

CHAPTER 4

Raise Your Fees Annually

MANY DENTISTS DO NOT get around to raising their fees annually or semiannually. I recommend that you routinely raise your fees 2% to 4% a year just to keep up with inflation and the rising cost of dental materials. Even though you are locked in by some insurance plans, you should routinely do this for all other patients.

Most owners do not understand the power of raising fees to increase net profit. If you have $100,000 per month practice and your overhead is 70%, your net profit would be $30,000 that month. A 10% increase in fees would give you an additional $10,000, when added to your net of $30,000, you would have a total net of $40,000. This is a 33% increase in your profit.

Below is a chart that shows you how a 1%, 3% and 5% increase could affect the total net income of your practice over thirty years. Go to ADA.org/feesurvey to get a free 2018 fee guide for your area. These are free for ADA members. You can also purchase the updated fee guide for your ZIP Code from Wasserman-medical. com for $169. Try to keep fees that the patients call about in the eightieth percentile. Because of dental insurance companies' pressures, you cannot collaborate to set fees with other dentists, but you *can* ask them what their fee guide is and then make your own decision regarding what your new fees will be. You may also hire someone to negotiate your fees with your insurance companies. (Check out Becky Balok at www.bbdentalconsulting. com.)

INCREASED NET PROFIT BY INCREASING FEES				
Totals	Yearly Collections	Total Collections Increase		
		1% per year	3% per year	5% per year
30 years	$500,000	$2,556,370	$9,501,339	$19,880,395
30 years	$1 million	$5,112,740	$19,002,678	$39,760,790
30 years	$1.5 million	$7,669,110	$28,504,017	$59,641,185

CHAPTER 5

Hire a Practice Management Expert

WHY WOULD ANYONE WANT to spend the money to bring in a dental consultant? The main reason, of course, is that what you're doing right now is not working. Doing more of it just becomes frustrating and exhausting. I think the big reason many dentists resist is that they are afraid to give up control of the practice, or that it might not work.

Many dentists have never taken the time to set up an efficient business model. To significantly increase practice profitability, hire a coach who is familiar with your type of practice (that may include areas such as sleep apnea, conscious sedation, Cerec crowns, etc.) or who has a good track record of success. Just by modifying a few things in a practice, dentists can often double their net profit. Remember, adding just one more crown per day increases your net profit by over $200,000 a year. Having systems in place to schedule patients more efficiently, doing same-day service, collecting fees at the time of service, emphasizing more profitable procedures, and raising fees are all examples of best practices that significantly increase the bottom line without raising overhead.

Most dental consultants can modify your business model so you work three or four days a week instead of five and take four to eight weeks off each year for vacation. Profitability increases to a point where the doctor can pay off all debt within three to seven years. This is accomplished through systems and creating an incredible story: retiring in practice. With this model, why would anyone ever want to retire?

Dentistry is changing rapidly, and many forces are causing stress. Some of the external forces over which we have no control are: more corporate offices, increasing overhead due to insurance companies controlling fee growth, more general dentists, fewer dentists retiring, and the big one—money spent on retail shopping, vacations and timeshares instead of maintenance dentistry. We need to learn to stop stressing over things we cannot control and focus on what we can control.

Things we *can* control are internal factors such as low production, doctor compensation, fewer patients, tougher cases, open schedules, no-shows, last-minute cancellations, student debt, office drama, and overwhelming administrative challenges. If your practice is not growing, it is declining. More than 70% of all practices declined over the past few years.

Many dentists are frustrated and stressed in their practice. They think attending a practice management course will help them clear these problems. The real problem is that they don't know what is really wrong, and what they can really fix. Many have already spent too many hours trying to control their practice. The most important service a practice management coach can provide is to determine those issues that are holding you back and help you correct the systems and team issues that plague your practice. This why the consultant must come to the office for a day to speak with the team and observe the office flow and schedule.

Most dental students pay over $100,000 a year for their education, which does not include *anything* about practice management or efficient systems. Yet they balk at paying a consultant $50,000 a year to change the practice and become much more profitable. They see the consultant's fee as an expense and not an investment. But in fact, your practice is the engine of your life where your money is made, and a lot of dentists' engines need to be repaired or tuned up. A good dental consultant can maximize the efficiency of that engine resulting in two times or more increase in your net profit. I have a different practice management consultant come in to my office every three to four years, and it has always resulted in increased profitability. Many of these companies will do a free objective analysis of your practice and help you understand where improvement is needed. Here are three I recommend: https://blatchford.com/ ; https://summitpracticesolutions.com/ ; https://www.whitehallmgt.com/. I have personally worked with each of these companies in my own practice and can highly recommend them. If you are interested in a consultant, I would interview each of them to determine which company would be best for your practice. Coaching can result in an increase in collections of $100,000 to $250,000 a year and more. And 75% to 80% of that increased collection is net profit. Once the practice's systems are changed and you increase your collections, it is rare to backslide. So, even conservatively, that one-time investment of $50,000 can result in an increase in collections of $1 million to $2.5 million over the span of ten years. This is why a practice consultant is called an *investment*.

Also check out All-Star Dental Academy (https://www.allstardentalacademy.com/).

More importantly, the doctor who uses a consultant is finally creating a practice that he or she loves, with an A-team and happy, enthusiastic patients and high profitability. Implementing the most successful coaching, the doctors can increase their vacation time by an additional two to four weeks a year and still increase productivity. Remember that Uncle Sam pays 35% to 50%

of the consulting fee; if you have a partner, you also split the investment with him or her. Most doctors pay off a consultant's fee in the first three to six months with increased collections. The two questions you must ask yourself after trying to change all the issues in your practice are, "How is what I am doing now working?" and "What is the true value of time with my family and time for myself?" Consulting helps you get peace of mind and your freedom.

WHERE DO I FIND A DENTAL CONSULTANT?

I would initially check with your friends and the most successful practices in your dental community who have used coaches and ask them how good their experience was and most importantly, what was the result from their coaching process. When selecting a consultant, it is important that you have a compatible philosophy of practice and that the consultant understands your needs and concerns.

Make sure any consultant you consider uses online monitors to help you understand and track your important numbers and monitor your progress. You must be clear about your own goals and believe that the consultant's philosophy will fit you and your team. So, give yourself permission to be your best, and to reach your and your team's full potential.

WHAT DO YOU LOOK FOR IN A CONSULTANT?

- Has significant experience working in the dental office
- Has significant experience working as a consultant
- Can show you the track record of results
- Can give you three to four references of dentists they have coached

- Understands your problems and gives you insights and suggestions
- Can help you become a better leader and help you give up control
- Has an extremely positive personality, not negative or condescending, and can create a strong working and teaching relationship with your team and team leaders
- Understands the numbers (and can teach you how to understand the numbers)
- Offers a program that is individualized, not cookie-cutter
- Comes to your office so there is no loss of your production time

IS COACHING RIGHT FOR YOU?

Very few dentists see coaching as an investment that can give them over 1000% return. Many more will sign up for help when they have enough pain. One famous quote was, "When the pain to remain the same exceeded the fear to change." If you are not ready to be open to new systems, be able to let go of control and empower your team, unable to fire a bad employee, or think you already know the answers, then you are not ready for coaching. Working with a coach requires the willingness to implement positive change for both you and your team. If you can face your fears and are open to change, the rewards are many. The greatest reward is your freedom in your personal and professional life. Transform your practice and you transform your life.

USE A CONSULTANT TO HELP YOU CREATE A RETIRE-IN-PRACTICE MODEL

In our culture, retirement has somewhat of a negative connotation indicating *old age, too old to work,* or *a reward for working hard for forty years.* I do not buy into this antiquated concept of retirement. By my definition, retirement is the time of many choices, opportunities and excitement. I believe you can begin your retirement when you're young through the concept of "retire in practice." This happens when you become debt-free which allows you to have unlimited choices for your life, even in your thirties, forties and fifties. One of those choices is to work one day less a week, thus allowing you to spend more time with your family when you are young. Another choice is to take more time off for travel, to teach, to create or enjoy your hobbies, or work on your bucket list. Ask yourself what is the message you are sending to your children about how to live life? Give them the example, throughout your life, of what real retirement (choices) looks like. A good consultant can show you how to increase your profitability, get out of debt early and work fewer days. They can also help you bring in an associate when the time is right.

Even though your practice is a constant source of income and can allow you to work as many days as you want, there may be a time when you are debt-free and financially free and would just like to sell your practice, work one or two days a week, or just walk away. There is no right answer, but you do have choices and the time to figure out what works best for you. You and your spouse need to create this story together.

Retiring in practice begins with a beautiful vision, the right systems, scheduling, great team, efficient techniques, and marketing. Once you become totally debt-free, which happens much sooner when you have increased your practice profitability, you can bring in an associate without reducing your net profit.

Hire a doctor who wants to be a long-term associate and does not want to have any of the issues involved with running a practice or ownership. They must be compatible with you and have your same treatment philosophy.

You can now drop to three days a week, be open five days, and take much more vacation time because your practice is covered. When you work fewer days, you are refreshed, do higher quality treatment, and enjoy your practice more. You create an empowered team that runs the practice, but you maintain complete control. Re-program your belief that you need to work hard. Be and live healthy while creating the adventure of your life.

Instead of selling your practice, bring in another associate and you come into the office four hours per month, just to check in with the team and review the numbers. This is called *retire-out-of-practice model*. You can take home half of your previous net without doing dentistry.

To do this you need an empowered team that runs the practice while providing an ideal patient experience through loyal associate doctors and motivated team members. To maximize the practice's success, work with a practice management consultant each year to ensure all systems are monitored, new team members are trained, and office leaders are supported to ensure the doctor's goals are met. Below is a chart of the retire in and out of practice model.

RETIRE IN/OUT OF PRACTICE MODELS				
	Working	**Retire in Practice 1**	**Retire in Practice 2**	**Retire Out of Practice (remote controlled practice)**
Practice Type	Solo Owner works 4-5 days/ week (190 to 225 days/ year)	Owner works 3 days/ week with one associate (130 days per year)	Owner works 2 days/ week with multiple associates (90 days per year)	Team managed with multiple associates and non-producing owner (0 days per year)

FIGURE 6

CHAPTER 6

Learn How to Invest Safely and Simply

ONCE YOU ARE DEBT-FREE, you need to know the safest places to invest your money without high risk and without management fees. This part of the book will give you a specific game plan to reach your investment goals. The greatest return on your investment always comes first from paying off debt and becoming more profitable in your practice. The next safest and guaranteed investment is in the creation of a Private Family Bank using a specialized whole life insurance policy that gives you a consistent guaranteed 4 percent plus return tax free. This is discussed in appendix D. Investing in the stock market may provide a higher nonguaranteed taxable return but is more volatile with higher risks. The return can be significantly increased when you learn to eliminate fees by investing on your own through one of the companies such as Schwab or Vanguard which I will discuss below.

DISCLAIMER

I have found the following investment information to be helpful. I am not engaged in rendering professional services. If you require personal assistance or advice, seek a competent professional. I specifically disclaim any responsibility for any loss, liability, or risk, personal or otherwise, which is incurred therefore directly or indirectly from the use and application of the contents of this book.

Many dentists get confused with investing and do not understand how easy it is to invest on their own through a company like Schwab or Vanguard. That is why they are so vulnerable to investment schemes and high-fee advisors and brokers. In this chapter I will give you the secret to simple investing. More in-depth detail will be found in Appendix D.

When I first started coaching dentists, I knew debt reduction and financial freedom were important. I also knew that people could achieve financial freedom easily. I had grand dreams about how I could make a big difference in people's lives. I developed the financial freedom guide through which they could accumulate gigantic amounts of money, and I showed them a sure and safe path to financial freedom. I had the illusion that in this way I could help my clients commit themselves to a safe economic pathway and change their lives.

I soon became discouraged, because many of my clients and their CPAs, brokers and financial advisors made a mess out of my finely designed plans. Instead of paying off debt, these "helpers" encouraged dentists to take their money and buy insurance, risky stocks, hedge funds, annuities and speculative real estate. They put their clients' assets into actively managed mutual funds that took 3% to 4% of their return for themselves, resulting in a 60% to 70%

loss of return that could have been made for my clients. The losses were in the millions of dollars in my clients' investment portfolios, thus preventing geometric progression of their retirement plans, and undermining my advice.

We seem to have an infinite capacity to stress ourselves, especially when it comes to money. To a large degree, this comes from greed and ego. I knew one dentist who took his entire retirement plan of $300,000 and put it into a limited partnership. He did not really understand the potential risks and rewards, and he had no control over them. Within one year, he lost his entire retirement nest egg that had taken him twenty years to earn. I know a very smart and skilled chiropractor friend who got involved in a "Bernie Madoff"-type scheme and lost his entire savings of $1.3 million that took him twenty years to accumulate.

I teach from my own life experiences and have probably made every financial mistake in the book, including day trading, buying an oil well over the phone for $5,000 that disappeared in a few months, buying timeshares, and buying land where I was never going to live. From my many life experiences, financial misadventures and my work as a dental coach and financial mentor, I have developed a consistent philosophy and a guide to investing that can work for anyone.

In my money context, I want to reach financial freedom as safely and quickly as I can. People have a wide range of economic strategies. Some spread out their money and lose it by placing it into various so-called investments such as insurance, risky stocks, hedge funds and speculative real estate, commodities, day trading, and limited partnerships, hoping they will strike it rich. For most dentists, these strategies are not efficient or reliable. Another strategy some people use is to reduce the amount of taxes they pay. Personally, I know that the more taxes I pay, the more money I am making. Americans have a history of hating taxes. One of the things that pushed us into the American Revolution was taxation by England without representation. So, it's not surprising that one popular economic program revolves around avoiding taxes. In the 1970s and 1980s, there were tax shelters that were really taxes in disguise.

Some people are so busy avoiding taxes that they lose sight of the goal of financial freedom. Some people buy larger houses than they need so they'll have more interest to write off on their taxes. Saving money on taxes is foolish if it costs more money than it saves.

Everyone in this country could become financially free if they spent less than they made, or made more than they spent, got out of debt and invested the difference in safe, liquid assets. If numbers and the idea of self-investing confuses you, this next paragraph will summarize all you need to know about successful investing. For a more in-depth understanding of investing, risk management and investment options, go to Appendix D.

Dr. Ace's Financial Freedom Guide
Simple Investing Summary

Make more money in your practice (use a coach) and focus all that money toward debt reduction. Once you are debt-free, create a Private Family Bank (https://smartestwealthsystems. com/PFB-for-dentists). This is a specially designed dividend paying whole life insurance policy where most of your premiums go into a rider that accelerates your growth of your equity and cash value in the policy. The plan reduces the commission the advisor receives by 50% to 70% and you will have up to 40 times more cash value, especially in the early years than with a traditional whole life policy. Because of the lower commission, most insurance agents do not offer this policy. These policies offer guaranteed tax-free growth and safety for your principal investment regardless of the ups and downs of the stock market or the economy. You will be able to use it as a financial management tool right from the beginning. This policy provides you tax-free access to your money for purchases, disability income or tax-free money for your retirement years giving you guaranteed growth that you can count on. The policy provides peace of mind and an income-tax-free legacy that you can pass on to your loved ones and/or favorite charities without going through probate. This is one of the safest, no risk investments for dentist. The next option that involves risk is investing in the stock market. You can increase your return by 1% to 4% by eliminating of the advisor and mutual fund fees when you learn to invest on your own. To do this create a Schwab account or a Vanguard account.

Both of these companies have great salaried advisors who will teach you how to invest on your own, step-by-step. Many of the "helpers" (brokers and financial advisors that you may have now) provide complicated investing strategies with multiple investment choices or investment theories such as Modern Portfolio Design, so you will think that investing is complicated and too hard for you to do alone. So you pay them high fees, even though their returns are less than the S&P 500 or US stock index. William Bernstein said, *"You are engaged in a life-and-death struggle with the financial service industry. Every dollar in fees, expenses, and spreads you pay them comes directly out of your pocket. Act as if every broker, insurance salesman, mutual fund salesperson and financial advisor you encounter is a hardened criminal, and stick to low cost index funds, and you'll just do fine."* So don't fall for that scam.

I was talking with my good dentist friend who had just recently married a beautiful lady whose husband died three years before. She related a story of a broker she went to for help with her investments which she knew little about. She was still dazed and confused from her loss and took all the funds she had gathered from selling homes, cars, dental practice and closing accounts. In December 2012, she gave the broker all her assets and asked him to "Manage this, be conservative, thank you."

He immediately placed her in an "actively managed account" and charged a 1% "wrap fee" annually, PLUS there were fees inside the account, e.g. front-end loads on mutual funds and high annual fees on mutual funds! In mid-2014, my friend and his new wife tried to get a handle on her returns, fees and commissions. They asked the financial advisor three questions: What was the returned in the managed portfolio in 2013? (Answer . . . +plus 5%.) What was the S&P 500 return for 2013? (The answer was ... plus 32.31%.) The third question was, how much were the total fees charged for the management of the portfolio for 2013? (The answer . . . $28,000.00!) This story is not uncommon in the brokerage world and demonstrates why we need to understand the simple concepts of investing safely.

If you are with a financial advisor or a mutual fund company that is charging you more than $1,000 to $4,000 per year, you are paying too much and should transfer assets to Schwab or Vanguard into a low-cost index funds. Remember that a 1% to 2% fee could reduce your retirement assets, so you will have to work another ten years. I personally use Schwab because they are open 24 hours a day, seven days a week, have no minimum balance to open an account, and all trades within their funds and ETFs are free. All other trades, no matter what the amount, are $4.95. This is a great place to put your children's money: Roth IRAs. Both Schwab and Vanguard make it very easy for you to transfer assets from your overpriced mutual fund company and advisor into their company.

Most of us do not like confrontation with our past advisor when we try to transfer our assets. However it becomes very easy when you call a Schwab representative and fill out the forms to have your assets automatically transferred into your new Schwab account. You don't even need to talk to your former advisor. To avoid the higher fees in your old company when you sell a stock or heavily loaded mutual fund, have the assets transferred to Schwab first, then sell them for only $4.95. When you transfer your account, ask for twenty free trades for opening your account. There may be a few mutual funds that they cannot transfer over, those will need to be sold into cash at your former brokerage house.

Now determine how much you need to diversify into US stocks, international stocks and bonds. This will depend on your risk tolerance and other factors. Appendix D will help you narrow your list of best individual asset allocation between bonds and stocks. For example, all you need to buy in your stock portfolio is the low-cost S&P 500 or total US stock market index mutual fund or ETF as described below. Then you're done.

Just buy the US market, never get out, and automatically keep buying each month and add extra when the market drops. You can buy the Schwab S&P 500 index ETF (ticker symbol SCHX) at the expense ratio of 0.03%, or the Vanguard 500 index ETF (ticker symbol VOO) with an expense ratio of 0.04%, both returning an average annual return over a ten-year period of about 11.9%. Or you can buy Schwab US Broad Total Market index ETF (ticker symbol SCHB) at the expense ratio of 0.03%, or the Vanguard Total Stock Market Index ETF (ticker symbol VTI) with an expense ratio of 0.04%, both returning an average annual return over a ten-year period of 12.1%.

Each month automatically transfer a set amount of money from your bank to your Schwab or Vanguard money market account. Always stay in the market and never sell, especially when the market drops: this is the time to buy more index funds. Today, at the beginning of 2019, the markets again are moving up or are at all-time highs. This is not the time to buy into the market. Remember the adage about buy low and sell high. Take advantage of market drops greater than 15% and buy the S&P 500 or the US stock market index using your money market account. Stop listening to the news and what's happening in the economy or the market. This is just noise. Don't even open your monthly investment statements. Check once a year in December when you give the statements to your CPA. If you want to have a 401k plan for your office, go to America's Best 401k plan. That's it, you're done. Now enjoy your life.

I know that an all-stock portfolio such as the S&P 500 index fund sounds risky, but because of recent low interest rates, the ten years' total bond funds returns averaged 3.4%, international stocks averaged 6.6%, and the S&P 500 averaged 13%. History has always shown that the S&P 500 index has had a consistently higher return over time as compared to bonds and international stocks. This is the fastest way to become financially free. If you want high returns, you are going to invest in stocks (S&P 500) and occasionally experience losses in the market — but only if you sell — and if you want safety you're going to invest in bonds and endure low returns.

I recommend that you do not start investing until you are debt-free, which increases your net worth and adds to the real estate portion of your portfolio. Because you maintain a good income, you can manage downturns in the market even if you have 100% of your portfolio in the S&P 500. If you choose to be in a stock-and-bond mixed portfolio, you could expect an annual return of 2% to 6% lower than the S&P 500 index fund. **Remember that a yearly loss of only 1%, either in market returns or in fees, could cost you well over a million dollars in your portfolio over 20 years.** What do you think a return of 6% less in your portfolio would cost you over 20 years?

Investing simplified: If you want high returns, you will need to take more risk (stocks) and occasionally must endure drops in the market, but if you want safety (bonds, T-bills, CDs, money market funds) you are going endure **low returns**. Historically, when the S&P 500 drops, it has always rebounded, so never sell.

When you are working, your steady income is like having a bond portion in your portfolio. Also, your paid off debt such as your home, your practice, and you're building are like a long-term inflation adjusted bond that is not affected by market corrections. These assets provide a source of emergency money through home-equity loans or lines of credit. Your income and these inflation protected assets allows you to invest 100% into equities (S&P 500) for the long term, which will give you the greatest rate of return.

We are not smart enough to beat the market, but all we need to do is match the market. Long-term, you may never need to touch the principal because if you love what you do you can easily fund your lifestyle by working part-time. If you completely retire you will be debt-free and have your Social Security, money from the sale of your practice, your 401(k) distributions, dividends from your stocks and possibly rental income allowing you to continue to invest in equities. Social Security is like owning a big inflation-indexed bond delivering a stream of income that rises with inflation. Because much or all of your living expenses are covered, you can have much more in your portfolio in stocks which you might not even use and eventually give to your family and charities of your choice. Go to Appendix D for a better understanding of different investment options and how to invest in the market on your own. You will also find recommendations for safer (low return) investments for those who are more fearful about downturns in the market. Each of us know how much risk we can take so that we can sleep well at night. Do the pillow test. If you lay your head on your pillow at night and you are thinking about your stock portfolio, then reduce the amount of equities in your portfolio until you can fall asleep peacefully. Appendix D will show you safe options where you can obtain financial freedom without taking significant risks.

At the beginning of the annual Berkshire Hathaway meeting in 2018, Warren Buffett wanted to share an important lesson with its shareholders. I will summarize what he said: *"Let's look back to 1942 when I bought my first stock and all the things that have happened since that time. We have had fourteen presidents, seven Republicans and seven Democrats. We had world wars, 9/11, Cuban missile crisis, and all kinds of terrible events that affected the market. But the best single thing you could have done on March 11, 1942 when I bought my first stock was to buy an index fund* (Buffett specifically mentioned the S&P 500 index fund) *and never ever look at another headline. Just like you would have bought a farm and let the tenant farmer run it for you and never sell it. If you had put in $10,000 in an index fund at that time and reinvested the dividends you would have $51 million today in 2018.*

If you took the same $10,000 and bought 300 ounces of gold, you would only have about $400,000 today. Gold does not produce anything, but businesses do. All you needed to do was to believe America would win the war and America would progress as it has ever since 1776. As America moves forward, American business moves forward. You didn't have to worry what stock to buy or what day to get in or out of the market or what the federal reserve would say. You just had to know that America works!"

When I was at Command and General Staff College back in 1981, we had the post commander, Lieut. Gen. Stone, speak to the entire cadre of the school one afternoon on finances. He told us get out of debt and invest in an IRA. At that time, the maximum you could put in was $2,000 so I took $4,000 and funded my IRA for 1981 and 1982 with a broker at Edward Jones. He put me into Putnam Voyager, a loaded mutual fund that I left in and never touched for 18 years. It had the same return as the S&P 500. From 1982 to the year 2000, I never looked at or worried about the investment. I was shocked to see my $4,000 had grown $105,000, an overall return of twenty-six times. That is the power of compound interest if you just let it ride and don't pay attention to it. I know two general dentists who produced no more than $1.2 million per year and used this exact strategy of getting out of debt and investing in S&P 500 and total US stock market index funds and retired in their sixties with a net worth well over $10 million.

INVESTMENT VEHICLES FOR PENSION PLANS AND IRAS

Once you are debt-free I highly recommend that you take advantage of the various tax deferred IRAs, pension and 401(k) plans that are available to you as a dentist. For a better understanding of what plans are available and for a comparison of plans go to: https://www.whitecoatinvestor.com/comparing-retirement-accounts/

In his recent book, *Unshakeable*, Tony Robbins spent a lot of time talking about how most companies that provide and manage 401(k) plans are ripping off the participants and owners of the plan. These plans are loaded with expensive mutual funds, excessive administrative expenses, and fat commissions to the brokers who sell the plan. In contrast, America's Best 401k is a company that offers only inexpensive index funds from firms such as Vanguard and dimensional fund advisors. Tom Zgainer, CEO of the company, charges only one fee with no markups or hidden costs. It is a full, bundled solution that eliminates brokers, commissions, and highly paid middlemen. He recommends investing with America's Best 401k to get the best returns at the lowest cost.

In addition to 401k plans, AB 401k also manages Cash Balance (CB) plans. When paired with a 401k, the CB plan allows for rapidly accelerated contributions while at the same time significantly reducing tax liability. These paired plans will generally work best when the dentist is older than 40 with a staff mostly younger than the dentist. I recommend you go to the website and use the company's free online Fee Checker tool at www.ShowMeTheFees. com. I have sent many of my clients to compare the fees at America's Best, and they have all moved their plans.

As an example, one of my dental clients who had about $1.4 million in her plan and added about $100,000 each year did a fee comparison. America's Best 401k total annual investment-related fees were 0.5%, compared to 1.73% in her original plan. If both plans got a 7% return over the next twenty years, the 1.23% difference in fees would have cost her $1.7 million in lost retirement savings. To look at this in another way, because of that 1.23% fee which would have resulted in a $1.7 million personal financial loss, she would have to work for another ten more years before retiring. Over a 30-year period the loss would be $4.93 million. How many more years do you have to work with a 3% advisor or actively managed fund fee? By eliminating the fees, it allows you to buy back the one thing that is limited in your life, which is your time on this planet. This is why it is essential that you compare your plans.

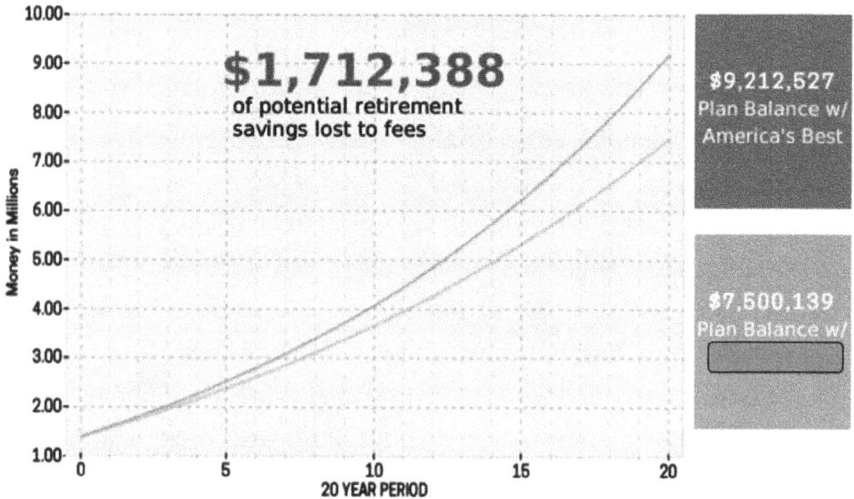

$1,712,388
of potential retirement
savings lost to fees

$9,212,527
Plan Balance w/
America's Best

$7,500,139
Plan Balance w/

20 YEAR PERIOD

IMPACT OF FEES ON BALANCE OVER TIME

Ending Balance	America's Best	Other plan	Increased Retirement Savings
Year 1	$1,597,054.67	$1,577,312.19	$19,742
Year 5	$2,526,285.66	$2,387,107.28	$139,178
Year 10	$4,083,417.55	$3,669,528.16	$413,889
Year 20	$9,212,526.80	$7,500,138.91	$1,712,388

FIGURE 7

ESTATE PLANNING AND ASSET PROTECTION CHECKLIST

Over 30% of the dentists I consult with do not have a will, power of attorney, or trust. Without these items, there is a great possibility that if something happens to you and your spouse, your drunken brother will take over all the money, spend it and throw your kids out on the street. Think about it. Without a revocable living trust, your estate will go into probate which makes all your assets public and is very expensive and emotionally draining to your heirs. It could take years before your estate is settled, thus depleting much of your estate's assets.

I was working with a thirty-four-year-old dentist who had a very nice practice, a little girl, and one more child on the way. I told him to go to his local attorney and get these estate planning documents drawn up. He said he would. Six months later, he was coming with his wife and team to one of my seminars in Seattle. During the flight, the plane had a landing gear issue and they thought they would have to make a crash landing in Seattle. Fortunately, they got the gear down and landed safely. At the meeting, I asked him, "Don't you feel better now that you have your asset protection plan in place?" He sheepishly said, "I will get those things done as soon as I get back."

Find a local attorney and get these things done now:

- Durable power of attorney for healthcare
- Durable power of attorney for finances
- Living will
- Standard will
- Revocable living trust
- Irrevocable trust

For a less expensive approach you can also go to LegalZoom and set up one for as little as $250 with the help of its attorneys. http://www.legalzoom.com/living-trusts/living-trusts-overview.html. Make sure to update beneficiaries on all your banking and investment accounts. The beneficiaries get first claim, and those listed on the will are secondary.

Recommended additional reading:

Dahle, James M., MD *The White Coat Investor: A Doctor's Guide To Personal Finance And Investing*. The White Coat Investor LLC.2014.

https://www.whitecoatinvestor.com/introduction-to-estate-planning/

https://www.thebalance.com/why-beneficiary-designations-override-your-will-2388824

Life Insurance. In the past I was a big fan of cheap term insurance as compared to a standard whole life insurance policy. But whole life insurance can be modified to create your own Private Family Bank and can be one of the best and safest places to invest your money without risk while receiving consistent predictable returns. To learn more about the Private Family Bank read John Cummuta's 2017 book The Banker's Secret to Permanent Family Wealth: Live your life . . . And build your wealth . . . using the same money. Most insurance salesman are unaware of this type of policy so for more information on the Private Family Bank designed for dentist contact: https://smartestwealthsystems.com/PFB-for-dentists

Disability insurance. I recommend that you go to the Eagleston financial group to evaluate all your insurance needs such as disability insurance. (http://eaglestonfinancialgroup.com/). I have worked with them for many years, they are extremely helpful and very honest.

Should you buy or rent a home? Bottom line: do not purchase a home until your student loans are all paid off and you have at least a 20% down payment. In 2019 the median home listing price in the US is nearly $280,000, according to Zillow, that varies by state. The average American moves every 7 years. By then, only 12% of the home is paid off. Then they get a new mortgage, starting all over again at 100%. With a $280,000 mortgage they have paid $34,257 toward their mortgage and lost $90,569 to the bank in interest during those seven years. They also paid an additional 6% in sales commission ($16,800), $10,000 in home improvements, plus $4,000 in closing costs. The bottom line is there was no increase in their net worth, and they will never ever get out of debt.

If they stay in the home and choose to pay back the original $280,000 loan at 4.9 % over the next 30 years, they will pay the $280,000 home price plus the $254,972 in interest, which equals $534,972 in after-tax money. I recommend that you never carry a mortgage larger than twice your gross income, and you should not spend more than 16% to 20% of your gross income on housing, including your mortgage payment, utilities, property tax, insurance and maintenance. Buy a home that is just large enough for your family and one you can afford to pay off in seven to ten years. Make sure you get a mortgage that has no penalty or fee for paying it off early. If you pay off the $280,000 home in seven years you would only need to pay $51,225 in interest and would save an additional $203,647 which would've gone to interest. Now you can use this money to invest in your retirement plan.

Remember: when buying a home over 30 years, most of the mortgage payments initially go to interest and very little goes to the principal (ownership) to pay off the home. For the first 15 years it is just like renting, except you have all the additional property taxes, maintenance, and homeowner's insurance. Beyond that, in most cases you can't even write off the interest on your taxes because they are less than the standard deduction. You are much better off renting until you have a 20% down payment (to eliminate the need for private mortgage insurance) and can plan to pay off the house in seven to ten years. Focus all excess money on those payments and don't dilute your extra money by paying into children's college fund or into your retirement unless it's matched by your employer. Once debt-free, you can invest in your children's college funding and other retirement plans. When you buy a home, you now have real estate in your portfolio and it becomes a form of forced savings, just like a long-term inflation-adjusted bond. Once paid off, that money which went to your mortgage payment now becomes like long-term dividends which can be invested more aggressively into the S&P 500 or total US stock market. Your paid-off home also becomes a safety net from which equity can be used in emergencies through home equity loans.

Unlike the dividends and interest from your investments, you don't have to pay taxes on inputted rent. This tax-free benefit is on top of the better-known tax breaks that home ownership enjoys, including the ability to take a tax deduction on the mortgage interest and property taxes, and to avoid capital gains tax on a big chunk of the profit when selling a home. In addition, when the market drops you just don't go out and sell your home like many investors do with their stocks.

The choice between buying a home and renting is among the biggest financial decisions that many adults make. I would recommend renting if you do not plan to live in the house for longer than seven years. Here is a calculator that uses the most important costs associated with buying a house and computes the equivalent monthly rent. https://www.nytimes.com/interactive/2014/upshot/buy-rent-calculator.html

Get rid of private mortgage insurance (PMI). If you did not have a 20% down payment when you purchased your house, you had to buy PMI, or private mortgage insurance. This is very expensive and can cost you up to 1% of the loan amount annually. A $400,000 house will require $4,000 a year in insurance payments, or $333 in monthly payments. In accordance with the Homeowners Protection Act of 1998, your lender must terminate PMI on the date your loan balance is scheduled to reach 78% of the original value of your home (in other words, when your equity reaches 22%, provided you are current on your mortgage payments). Call your lender and ask the lender to cancel your PMI when you have paid down the mortgage balance to 80% of the home's original appraised value. You might have to write your lender a cancellation letter of the

PMI. Accelerate your payments as fast as you can to eliminate the PMI and, once you've done this, you'll have an additional $333 a month to pay off your home early. https://www.investopedia.com/mortgage/insurance/how-get-rid-pmi/

FINANCIAL MYTHS AND MISTAKES

Over the years, we have been imprinted with financial myths. Once we look closely at them, we realize how they are wrong and keep us from reaching our financial goals. Below, I will address a few of these beliefs and recommend you see them for what they are: myths. Also check out: https://www.whitecoatinvestor.com/stupid-doctor-tricks-biggest-financial-mistakes/

- **Myth 1: Good debt versus bad debt.** Some people say that your house or your business are good debt. But all debt is bad and sucks the life out of your financial world. We must remember that debt is the devil! Get rid of it as soon as possible. Becoming debt-free uncomplicates your life.

- **Myth 2: Pay yourself first and start saving for your retirement**. The problem with doing this is that you're only getting less than 1% return in your savings account when instead, you could use that money and get over 100% return right now by paying off debt, which is the fastest way to become wealthy.

- **Myth 3: Why pay off a 3% interest rate home loan when I can make 7% investing?** We must remember that we are really getting over 100% return by paying off our principal payment on our loans. And again, who says we are going to get 7% in the market? In some years, the market has dropped by 35%.

- **Myth 4: Buy the most expensive house you can afford**. This just keeps you in debt longer and adds many more expenses to your life. The more expensive the house, the more you will pay in property taxes, home maintenance, home upgrades, yard maintenance, and (if you live in such a neighborhood) community dues. You now must upgrade your lifestyle to keep up with the neighbors. Instead, buy someone *else's* dream house that fits your needs. You will save 20% versus building your own house and sidestep the headaches of construction. Dr. Doug Carlson says that home maintenance, property taxes, and upgrades average 2% of your home's value per year for a modest home. Thus, a $500K home will need $10,000 per year. Unfortunately, that peripheral cost of 2% will increase with a more expensive home. Often, you'll pay 3% for a $1.5M home and over 4% for a $2M+ home. Yes, doctors can pay $80K and up each year for their "trophy" home. In Chapter 5, Dr. James M. Dahle, the author of *The White Coat Investor*, gives some good reasons why renting a home has its advantages during certain times in your career. Go to: https://www.whitecoatinvestor.com and type in "should I buy or rent?"

- **Myth 5: Emergency fund myth.** Some financial advisors recommend saving three to six months of living expenses in an emergency fund before you start paying off debt. The problem with this approach is that you never get around to paying off the debt, because it takes about two years to save up that amount, meanwhile, many people take out the money for nonemergency items. You must begin to see debt as a tax, and automatically pay 10% to 20% of your monthly income toward your debt. Once your credit cards are paid off, you do have an emergency fund, you can get a line of credit, home equity loan or you can just stop paying those accelerated payments for one or two months.

- **Myth 6: The budgeting myth.** Again, many good financial advisors recommend you observe where you're spending your money and then budget so much each month, which allows you to set aside money to pay off debts. The problem is this gives you a false sense of security and there is usually nothing left at the end of the month. The secret of debt elimination is to automatically take 10% to 20% out of your bank account each month to pay off debt as if it were a tax. I can guarantee you if you take 10% to 20% out each month and pay toward debt, you will be broke at the end of the month just like you are now, except you will be well on your way to becoming debt-free.

- **Myth 7: College funding myth**. Many people recommend you start funding your child's education early, so that you have enough when they're ready for school. They might recommend 529 plans that are run by different states, which have high-load, actively managed funds. The returns are dismal. You also have less control over the money. It is better to focus on debt reduction when debt-free, you can easily fund your children's college education with cash. When you are debt free and you want to start a 529 plan, check out **savingforcollege.com** for the best plans in all states.

- **Myth 8: The "more money" myth.** I've heard so many doctors say, "If I just had more money . . . "

When I first began my coaching program, I showed dentists how to make more money, but I forgot to teach them about getting out of debt. They just got into larger amounts of debt and are now trapped in their large homes and large high-stress lives. More money will not make you happy, but if you are focused on eliminating your debt, your life will become much more stress-free.

- **Myth 9: Life insurance as an investment.** This may be true with the standard whole life insurance policies that are regularly sold but with a highly modified whole life insurance policy it could be one of your best investments. Most insurance salesman are unaware of this type of policy so for more information on the Private Family Bank designed for dentist contact: https://smartestwealthsystems.com/PFB-for-dentists

- **Myth 10: Monthly payments are normal**. Our culture has taught us that we always need to be in debt. This makes a lot of money for many people in the banking and investment industries. So, stop paying them 100% interest.

- **Myth 11: Avoid-paying-taxes myth**. Dentists lose money by trying different schemes to prevent paying taxes. You should want to *pay more taxes than any other dentist,* because it indicates you are *making more money than any other dentist*. Rely on your CPA. A good CPA will keep you honest and make sure you don't give more to the government than you need to.

- **Myth 12: Financial advisor myth**. There is an old saying, "a broker will invest your money until you are broke." In the past, it was much more complicated to invest in the markets because people had to go to different brokerage houses and work through brokers. With the internet, it is easy to create an account online and find low-load index funds that will beat 96% of all the financial advisors because of the minimal 1% to 3% to manage your investments. Remember, a 1% advisory fee could cost you $1.5 million over twenty years if you had a $1.2 million 401k and you contributed $72,000 per year with an 8% return. For non-retirement money, use the free Schwab advisors and contribute each month into the S&P 500 index fund.

- **Myth 13: Myth of bi-weekly mortgage payments.** It is true that paying your mortgage twice a month will cause a 30-year mortgage to be paid off in about twenty-two years and save 25% of the interest. This strategy creates a false sense of security and keeps you from getting totally out of debt, including paying off the home, in five to seven years and saving 80% of the interest.

- **Myth 14: Don't pay off your house early because you can write off the interest rate on your taxes.** One of the biggest misconceptions that banks and accountants perpetuate is that you should not pay off your house early because you can write off the interest on your taxes. If we look at this closely, in 2018 an average American couple who pays $10,000 a year in interest has the choice of either taking the standard deduction of $24,000 or to itemize their return and take the $10,000 tax write-off. When they itemize, they are unable to take the standard deduction of $24,000 and have an overall loss of $14,000.

AVOIDING FINANCIAL MISTAKES

Warren Buffett said; "the first rule of investment is, don't lose money. The second rule of investment is, never forget rule number one." The most important way to keep your wealth is to never make a big financial mistake. Big financial mistakes usually occur because of greed and ego. I have known numerous dentists who have lost their entire portfolio in a get-rich-quick scheme. Such schemes range from real estate deals to limited partnerships; they can take the form of just about anything else that sounds too good to be true. Remember, *there is no free lunch.* When you have a systematic guide to get out of debt, increase your practice profitability, and conservatively invest in the US market, then you will become economically free in a fairly short time. Why take a risk on anything else? If you just stick with the boring *Dr. Ace's Financial Freedom* philosophy of investing, you'll never put your retirement money at risk. Here are some other financial mistakes you should avoid.

- **Not stopping to find out what makes you happy.** The things that really make me happy are very simple and cost almost nothing. If I had known this earlier at the deepest level, I would not have needed to drive myself so hard to be successful. This is why the process of writing a new story is so important. Write down what you want your average day to look like. What are the things that make you happy? (Don't include shopping!) What are the happiest times you've enjoyed in your life? When you know who you are, it is easy to save money. Usually the simplest and least expensive things make you happy. Try to spend the least amount of money trying to figure out what makes you happy. Rent your way through the discovery process (for example, rent that lovely condo in the mountains rather than buy it). Most people live a life of high debt and stress because they spend money hoping it will make them happy. I guarantee that more money or things will not give you peace or happiness.

- **Allowing our ego to ruin our lives** by creating an unconscious compulsion to enhance one's identity through association with and purchase of expensive items, i.e. jewelry, exotic cars, and luxury homes. Yet, rarely do these purchases satisfy the ego desires that make one feel different and special.

- **Lending money to friends and family.** If you lend money to friends or family, please realize there is a good possibility you will never be repaid. Often this has a negative impact on the relationship. If lending the money is meaningful to you, then consider simply giving it as a gift. Never cosign a loan; in most cases, you will end up paying the loan. A cosigner is a fool with a pen.

- **Falling for get-rich-quick schemes and scams.** Never get involved in any investment that you don't completely understand. With this guide, you do not have to take risk. You already have it made. When you are asked to invest in something new, just tell them that you only invest no-load S&P 500 or the US stock market, but thanks anyway. Check out: https://www. whitecoatinvestor.com/12-rules-to-help-you-avoid-getting-scammed/

- **Listening to investment financial advisors** who say they can beat the market. Only a fool would say they can beat the market, so just stick with no-load index funds that you can buy yourself.

- **Getting into a limited partnership**. You lose control as a limited partner and are the last to be paid. Stay away from any investment or thing that you do not understand thoroughly or do not have personal control regarding decisions.

- **Living in a high-cost, high-congestion and high-tax area.** If you to work and live in a large city like San Francisco or New York City where homes can be two to three times more expensive, you will find that traffic is terrible and there are high state and city taxes that can delay your becoming debt-free and financially free. Think about moving to a tax-free state such as Texas, Florida, Wyoming, Washington, Alaska, New Hampshire, South Dakota, Tennessee or Nevada. Live in a smaller, less expensive and hectic community, and affording you the option to buy a nicer and bigger home that you can pay off in five to seven years.

- **Buying too big a house.** Consider what you really need. Buying a bigger house than you need wastes money monthly. The cost of your home should not exceed two times your gross salary.

- **Buying a vacation home or large boat that you rarely use.** If this adds meaning to your life and you use it often, like more than sixty days a year, then it is worth the investment. That is, until it no longer adds meaning to your life—and at that time, you can sell it. It is not a bad idea for some properties like vacation homes or boats to be shared with other owners to dilute the expenses.

- **Buying timeshares.** Never buy them. You have a greater selection and a lot less price if you go to vacation rental by owner (VRBO.com).

- **Buying annuities**. Never buy them.

- **Starting another business** before you start making your own practice successful. A well-run dental practice can be one of the most successful businesses on this planet. Maintain your focus and start having fun again in your practice.

- **Marry the right person the first time**. Stay away from spenders. Find someone who is conservative in their spending habits and has financial goals similar to yours.

- **Not getting a prenuptial agreement if you have assets.** Get your spouse (male or female) to sign on the dotted line before you say "I do."

- **Having too many "successful" marriages.** Before divorcing, try to reinvent your relationship and work through a counselor to see if you can make the relationship work. If there is no possibility of working it out, then you both deserve your freedom. There's often a lot of anger and trying to "get even" in the divorce process. I recommend you offer your spouse a generous settlement and treat her/him with kindness and respect. Always try to maintain strong relationships with your children; never put down your partner. If your spouse wants more and does not accept your generous offer, then tell your attorney that his or her job is simply to get you in front of the judge and no longer communicate with your spouse's attorney. This will save both of you a lot money in attorney fees. Judges are normally fair in their settlements. If you continue to marry the same type of person (alcoholic, codependent, crazy), then this is the time for some personal growth and counseling.

CHAPTER 7*

Enjoy Life, Liberty, and the Pursuit of Happiness

*The Most Important Chapter

ENJOYING GOOD HEALTH

About three years ago I noticed that my computer IT guy had lost a considerable amount of weight. He was six foot two, and when I first met him, he weighed around 300 pounds. Within six months, he had dropped 100 pounds and now looked great. I was amazed because I disliked exercise and had always had trouble losing weight, so I asked him what his secret was.

He told me that weight loss was pretty much 90% diet and 10% exercise. He said he changed his eating habits and moved to a high-fat, low-carbohydrate, ketogenic method of eating. He recommended a site called Dietdoctor.com, which was founded in 2011 and has over 55,000 members worldwide, making it the largest low-carb site in the world. It is filled with many articles, experts, videos, and low-carb recipes.

At that time, I was five foot six and weighed about 200 pounds, with a beautiful pot belly. Within three months of taking his advice, I lost over thirty-five pounds and have maintained my weight at 165 pounds for the past three years. I walk a couple of miles once a week and do some weightlifting two times a week to keep my muscle tone. I take multivitamins, vitamin D, magnesium, and fish oil. I can now sleep eight hours a night, and I feel better than I have for years.

Another great website to help transform your health is http://drhyman.com/. Dr. Mark Hyman is an American physician and a *New York Times* bestselling author. He is the founder and medical director of the Ultra Wellness Center and director of the Cleveland Clinical Center for Functional Medicine. His books and audios on understanding functional medicine can change your life. See Appendix A.

CREATING GREAT RELATIONSHIPS

Warren Buffett gives the following advice. *"Be around people that you admire and enjoy. They usually have an upbeat attitude about life, they're humorous, have integrity and are generous people who are thinking about what they can do for you. These qualities that you admire are not innate at birth, and you can acquire them. Then there are those negative qualities that turn you off in people who always need to be right and that you don't enjoy being with. You can choose what person you want to be, so why not choose the person you admire? Take your five best friends, mentors or your heroes, and write down the qualities that you like about them. Incorporate these qualities in your life and eliminate the qualities of the people that turn you off. It's that simple. It is important to work with people in your life and you will get the best out of people if they like you. You need to develop these habits now. Incorporate the great qualities now and eliminate the bad qualities and you will have an incredible life. Choose your heroes very carefully because they will define you. You are one of your children's favorite heroes."*

Buffett also said that the secret to long-lasting relationships is low expectations. A friend told me that relationships improved immensely when you give up the need to be right. My wife, Nancy, and I were married in 1969. We have five children and thirteen grandchildren. We have had our ups and downs, but we are very supportive of each other. And if she has a problem that I know I can fix immediately, I listen intently and never offer advice. (There is a great and funny YouTube clip called *"It's Not About the Nail"* that makes this point very clear.)

Another great book is *The Five Love Languages,* by Gary Chapman. The five love languages are words of positive affirmation, acts of service, receiving gifts, quality time, and physical touch. Because I was abandoned as a child, my language is positive affirmation. This will fill up my love tank, while criticism will empty it. Even though I do some stupid things sometimes, Nancy is not critical of my errors. My wife's love language is quality time and acts of service. If she has something for me to do, such as change the burnt-out light bulb in the kitchen, I immediately do it.

When I see my underwear drawer full, I know she did the laundry, and I thank her. I often tell her how beautiful she is and how much I love her. Even though our children may do things that we do not like, we provide advice only when asked, are never judgmental or critical, and are there to love them no matter what happens in their lives. Warren Buffett said he never met a truly successful person who did not have a great relationship with their children. Are you truly successful?

One last comment: I would never be in a relationship that is toxic or does not add true meaning to my life. Sadly, this toxicity could be from parents who are always judgmental and critical of you. Tell any toxic person that if they continue to be judgmental or critical you will not be seeing them. I give you permission to take care of yourself first, or else you will not be good to anyone else. Think about what you are teaching your children about the type of relationship they should be in.

CREATING LOVE IN YOUR LIFE

Love is that special feeling we get when we have a connection with people and things in our life. It is created when we initiate and give love to people and things. Somebody could love us, but we may not feel anything, but we always feel love when we are loving others. We are fortunate to be in a profession where we can love our patients, our team, what we do and especially our family. This doesn't just apply to loving people but also things in our lives such as a good movie, a book, a special mug and other things we go back to and create that feeling of love. Like the movie, "Love Actually" is all around us.

TEACHING YOUR CHILDREN ABOUT FINANCES

Mahatma Gandhi was asked what his message to the world was. He said, "My life is my message." Teach your children the satisfaction of being a saver instead of a spender. You need to show them the satisfaction of accomplishment and doing a job well. Be the example for them of how they can find fun and joy in everything they do, instead of teaching them duty, responsibility and that you must work hard for living.

Teach your children to understand the ideas in this book. Create a job for them in your office so that they can fund a Roth IRA. Schwab is a great place to put this money because there is no minimum to open an account and are no fees when trading among their funds and ETFs. Any money your child makes, you can match. When the children are old enough, age ten or eleven, teach them the simple investing approach found in this book. William Bernstein, in his book, *The Investor's Manifesto,* suggests you set up a small portfolio with index funds in each child's name. Teach them how to file their account statements, log in and print out reports. Every quarter, set up an investment meeting with them and discuss portfolio performance. The most important thing you can leave your heirs will not be cold, hard cash, but rather the ability to save, spend and invest prudently. Reward them with the dividends and half of the capital appreciation of their stock funds. Let them experience both the ups and downs of the market and help them with their emotions showing them stocks that just came on sale. Andrew Tobias, in Chapter 10 of his book, *The Only Investment Guide You'll Ever Need*, has some great ideas on teaching your children about finances.

I knew one dentist who helped his daughter fund her IRA each year from age one by using the money she earned as a model for pictures in his office. He later had her work in his practice. By age thirty, they had put in $101,500 and her Roth IRA was worth over $450,000.

FINDING HAPPINESS

When we get to be between forty and fifty years old, our lives change. Many of us go through a clinical depression because we have lost the excitement of starting our careers or our practices. Things may be going smoothly. The kids may be in college. But life changes, even if we don't want to admit it. We don't make changes in our work life anymore, and we don't care if it gets any better; we just hope it doesn't get any worse. Sometimes we take up hobbies instead of creating excitement in our work lives. As we reach midlife, it's time to realize that this is it; it's not going to get any better; it's all in our minds. We need to recognize this is as an opportunity to go to work happy every day, and to change our relationship to work so that it is fun. Life can be exciting if we let it be.

The future does not exist except in our imaginations, and the past is merely a trace in our minds. The brain changes our recollections to fit our own convenience and purposes. This is also true with our work lives. Once we understand that we are working on a day-to-day basis, not a year-to-year basis, our attitudes and philosophies change, and incidentally, we become more prosperous and have more fun.

I have consistently found that those who were happy while they were working are also happy during their retirement years. The opposite is also true: those who did not enjoy their work don't find happiness in retirement any more than they did while they were working.

The life and business coach, Kendrick Mercer, once had a fifty-year-old client from North Carolina. The client told him he had hated dentistry for the past twenty-five years. The worst problem was that he could not quit because he owed so much money. Kendrick told him he could set up his finances to be economically free in ten years, but he knew his client's problem was deeper than finances, so he asked him, "Once you reach financial freedom, what are you going to do?"

"I would first quit my practice," the client told him.

"Then what are you going to do?" Mercer asked.

"I am going to golf," he replied.

"Then what are you going to do?" Mercer asked.

He said, "I will buy a place on the beach and walk on the beach."

"Great," Mercer said. "Then what are you going to do?"

"Then I will watch TV and read books."

"Then what are you going to do?" Mercer asked him one more time.

He became sad and somber and said, "I will just walk on the

beach some more."

"Great! What are you going to do then?"

He started to cry and said, "I'm going to die."

This is a pretty sad story. There was no real aliveness to this man, just a dead story. Mercer's fifty-year-old client was trying to get someplace instead of loving his life.

Mercer told him, "My job is to assist you in knowing that life is never going to be any better or worse than it is right now. It's just how you're looking at it. For you to go back and spend one more day losing your life for some future time which does not sound all that exciting will make your life a failure."

The client did not like hearing this, but he knew it was true. Mercer told him to go home and change his mind and outlook so he could enjoy dentistry again, and appreciate his patients, his staff, and all his relationships. If he did this and still did not enjoy dentistry, then he should quit, sell everything and do something with his life that he enjoyed.

The dentist friend did go back and created a new story for himself and his practice, then he began to enjoy his practice. Kendrick coached him to slow down and sell some things to get rid of his debt. The client finally started to relax. Because life is lived in the present, it will truly never get any better or worse than it is this minute. It's all a matter of how we look at our experiences. This principle is the same for each one of us.

I know dentists who have become debt-free and financially secure. Yet many tell me they are not happy. What I learned from Kendrick Mercer is that we carry many family imprints, negative emotional experiences such as abandonment or abuse, that make us feel we are not worthy of happiness. We need to address these issues and let go of the loss and pain from the past. Sometimes, we need counseling to help us through this process.

One company that I have worked with which has helped me and many doctors and their team members in identifying what holds them back from enjoying and finding peace in every aspect of their lives, resulting in more peace and happiness, is Legacy Life Consulting (http://legacylifeconsulting.com/).

IT'S NEVER TOO LATE

You may be in your 50s or even 60s and feel stuck in your practice, and in your life. Just like the story above, you can reassess your practice and life, and make changes now. I've worked with many dentists in their 50s and 60s helping them through the process of making their practice more efficient and fun while working fewer days. We also talked about getting rid of the junk in your life. Junk is defined as anything that does not add meaning to your life.

First, find out what your net worth is by writing down all your assets and debts (appendix B). Look at your practice and eliminate everything that does not make it fun. This may include team members who are negative and cause you drama. Eliminate and refer out all procedures that cause you stress, such as extractions or root canals. Write a letter to the 20% of your patients that cause you 80% of your grief. Set them free from your practice while providing a certain amount of days for emergency care. Each state's dental association will have an example of this letter that you can use. Before you begin the process, you may want to hire a practice management consultant to help you. This consultant can help you become much more efficient in your practice and may recommend procedures to control other conditions, such as sleep apnea, which can become a profit center. Once you become much more profitable, you could decide to sell your practice and move to a different part of the country where it may be warmer or where you can be closer to your children and work part-time. When you clear your mind and are open to all possibilities, the choices become endless.

As you go through this process, make sure you have your spouse on board. Some of the junk you may want to eliminate may include the large boat you only use two to three weeks out of the year but costs you $1000 in slip fees and maintenance each month. You may have had a loss in an individual investment such as a stock or limited partnership. Realize you already have taken the loss, and chances are great that it will never come back. However by you keeping this loss it distracts you from moving on and learning from your lesson. So just sell it and use the loss to offset your gains in other investments. The only exception are stocks that drop during a down market, because you *never* sell in a down market. You may have rental property that causes you a lot of headaches and low financial returns. It may be the large house with high maintenance costs which you could sell and move into a new or smaller home or condo and invest the difference in your retirement account. Go through your closet and get rid of all clothes and shoes that you have not worn in the past year. Getting rid of junk in your life gives you great peace of mind and contentment. Now you can focus on creating strong relationships with your spouse and your children.

WHAT PERCENTAGE OF YOUR CURRENT INCOME DO YOU NEED IN RETIREMENT?

Many financial advisors tell you you need 70% of your current income to be comfortable in retirement. I think one reason they say this is to make sure you keep investing more money in their actively managed funds. You will probably only need somewhere between 25% to 35% of your current income. Let me summarize an excellent article by Dr. James Dahle in his website, White Coat Investor. https://www.whitecoatinvestor.com/Percentage-of-current-income-needed-in-retirement/

Do the math: Take your current income, let's say $200,000.

Subtract out 20% for taxes and 20% for retirement and you're down to $120,000.

Subtract out 5% for insurance, 5% for child-related costs, and 15% for your mortgage. You're now down to $70,000. Subtract out another 1% for job-related expenses, 2% for reduced charitable contributions, and 1% for reduced housing expenses. You're down to $62,000.

Add back in, say, 10% for increased travel costs and 5% for increased health care costs. This moves us up to $92,000. Subtract out $36,000 for Social Security and that leaves us at $56,000, or 28% of our current income. Using the 4% rule, $56,000 per year, adjusted for inflation, can be provided by retirement assets of $1.4 million. How long will it take for you to reach that goal if you save 20% of your $200K income a year and get a return of 5% real return on it? Around 21 years.

THE ILLUSION THAT MONEY WILL MAKE US HAPPY

Most Americans fall prey to the illusion that money will make us happy. There are more miserable, depressed, and anxious millionaires than you can imagine! I've seen clearly and repeatedly that money will *not* buy happiness. Nothing that money can buy will make you happy on an ongoing basis, and many people resent those who have money. This attitude will prevent them from creating abundance in their lives.

The belief that money will make us happy seems almost unstoppable. It is one of the big illusions that keeps us from developing integrity with money. Some people think if they win the lottery, they will be happy, but things never seem to work out that way. Money can make people miserable because of their false expectation of what it will bring. What makes us happy is having integrity in every aspect of our lives, including expressing our feelings through travel, love, and relationships.

On some level, we all know money will not make us happy, but we still act *as if* it will. Money does bring a certain kind of security that we wouldn't otherwise have. With that security, perhaps we can express happiness or enjoy life more consistently. But being financially secure is different from being rich.

Happiness comes from enjoying each moment and appreciating everything that comes into our lives. It comes from helping others, such as our patients, our teams, and all others around us. This is where the real fun is. As we give love to others, we can't stop the abundance of love that comes into our own lives.

No precise dollar amount translates into this capacity. On the other hand, poor money management (such as having high debts and many creditors) can make you unhappy, that is one good reason for developing a clear financial context. Sometimes it takes buying the things you always thought you wanted to realize that they alone do not bring you happiness. Spending without a clear guide diffuses and wastes your money and your financial freedom. If you have a clear context about money, you'll rent the boat or vacation home you've dreamed of first, to see if it really does add meaning to your life.

Jonathan Clements, in his must-read book, *The Little Book of Main Street—Money: 21 Simple Truths That Help Real People Make Real Money,* says that buying things might bring us happiness but not long-lasting happiness. Over the past decades we have made vast improvements in our standard of living, yet people still aren't any happier. We need to get off the treadmill and think about how we spend our money and how we spend our time. Clements makes six recommendations for happiness.

Buy experiences rather than things.

Count your blessings.

Strive for a sense of control.

Find a purpose instead of trying to have endless leisure.

Give a little, volunteer or donate.

Make time for friends and family.

His website has a wealth of information that is always updated and worth visiting. https://humbledollar.com/money-guide/main-menu/

STOP COMPLAINING.

Half of the people think you deserve what you get, and the other half don't care. Kendrick Mercer shared a story with me after his three-month sailing from California to Lahaina, Maui. His trip was an incredible adventure with beautiful sunny days, stormy weather, moonbows at night and wonderful solitude. After arriving in Lahaina, he took a plane to Honolulu. He was enjoying the view over the ocean while a lady sitting next to him was complaining to him about her life, children and husband. During the break in her conversation he looked at her and said, "Let's play a game. Let's pretend the plane breaks right in half and we are all going to die. All you see in front of you is blue sky. We have two choices: we can grab on to the armrest in terror and think about all the things we didn't do in our life, or we can calmly unbuckle our seatbelts, stand up, jump forward and fly for the rest of our lives." She did not say much after that but gave him a big hug at the end of the flight. Why not live our life in gratitude and enjoy every moment?

CULTURAL AND FAMILY IMPRINTING

I realized that before my clients could be at peace with money, they had to open and address the deeper behavioral issues keeping them from having integrity with money and with life.

Our attitudes toward money can keep us from living full and peaceful lives. We have all inherited a range of imprints from our families of origin concerning money. These imprints often including prejudices, insecurities, and false assumptions, which pull us away from developing integrity with money. We tend to repeat the clichés about money that we learned as children, even if they're not true, such as "You can never have enough money," "It takes money to make money," "The poor working man can never get ahead," and "You must work hard for your money."

Most people who have plenty of money keep working, not because they enjoy it or choose to, but because working has come to represent worthiness. It is a kind of cultural fad. Work seems to justify our very right to exist. The family imprint duty, responsibility and working hard for a living, may be incredibly strong, or perhaps work has become an addiction. Many people work because that is what society expects them to do, or because their parents told them they'd be bums if they didn't work hard six days a week. Our current attitudes about money tend to limit our choices even when we have achieved wealth. The ideal balance would be to have a great deal of money and at the same time to be at peace, doing only what we really want to do. For most of us, our lives are half over, and it is time to have some fun now! You cannot create what you cannot envision. Get very clear about making your life fun and enjoyable; feel it and keep moving toward that vision. Bring your vision to your office and your family, don't settle for anything less. Take time to talk to your children not about duty or responsibility, but about what brings happiness, fun and joy into their lives, and what it will take to create that story for them.

HOW DO WE DEFINE SUCCESS?

This can be different for each one of us. For me, it is about loving what I do each day, being at peace in my life, being in good health, having time to be with and enjoy people I love, being debt-free, having enough money that I don't worry about money anymore, and having the time and resources to make a difference in the world around me. Others may define success as being the best dentist, making a lot of money, having time to do missionary work, retiring at age fifty-five, having $7 million in the bank, the list goes on. This book is not meant to define your success, but to show you how to have enough time and money to make choices in your life that are right for you. It's not about making a living, it is about making a life worth living.

French writer François-René de Chateaubriand (1768 to 1848) said, *"A master in the art of living draws no sharp distinction between his work and his play; his labor and his leisure; his mind and his body; his education and his recreation. He hardly knows which is which; he simply pursues his vision of excellence through whatever he is doing, and leaves others to determine whether he is working or playing. To himself, he always appears to be doing both."*

HOW MUCH IS ENOUGH?

If you are like most people of the world, one bowl of rice a day would be enough. Here in America we think in terms of economic freedom. In my past book, *Time and Money,* I define economic freedom as the day you have accumulated enough safe, liquid assets that can reproduce your lifestyle income (the amount of money it takes to maintain your lifestyle), with safeguards against inflation, for the rest of your life without touching the principal. This will vary by individual, but once you are debt-free you could reach that point in five to seven years, by simply following the recommendations in this book.

MAKE A DIFFERENCE IN THE WORLD

There is difference between success and significance. One of the great advantages of having more time and more money is to make a difference in the lives of people in the world around us. One reason I enjoy going into the office two days a week is that I can create such abundance to share with others. Each year, I donate to many great causes including the Union Gospel Mission dental clinic for our street people, Safe Place for battered women, the food banks, a dental assisting program, my church and various other causes that make a difference in the world around me. I do believe that this even brings more abundance into my life. Even though you are working on paying off debt, donate either your time or money to an important cause. This will make a difference in your life and those you help.

THE TWO-DOLLAR-BILL STORY OF HAPPINESS

I love giving out two-dollar bills as reminder of our freedom in the United States. This $2 bill is the only piece of US currency that depicts the same person on the front and on the back. On the front of the bill, we see Thomas Jefferson, the third president of the United States. Then we turn the bill over and him signing the Declaration of Independence. The people standing around the table are the committee who wrote the declaration. The main author is Thomas Jefferson (the tall person in the center). The person standing on the far left is John Adams, the second president of the United States.

John Adams and Thomas Jefferson had a few things in common: They were both presidents and were the only presidents who signed the Declaration of Independence. They both died on July 4th, within three hours of each other, exactly fifty years after they signed the Declaration of Independence.

FIGURE 8

In those days, the average man lived to age thirty-five. Adams was ninety and Jefferson was eighty-three on the day they died. I believe the reason they lived two to three generations beyond the average man is that they were both highly motivated to instill and imprint the ideals of freedom and independence into our American culture. They lived with a purpose.

This is why we live in one of the freest countries in the world and can work and live anywhere we want in this country. We are free to be in any mutual relationship we want, and to leave it if it is toxic (a relationship where you will never grow and are always being put down).

Sadly, most Americans don't know they are free. Many feel trapped in their lives, practice, jobs and relationships. They feel angry, controlled, frustrated, anxious or sad. These feelings come from a place of fear—many people fear change and have one foot in and one foot out of their choices (relationships or jobs).

These feelings immediately disappear when the person acts, after choosing to change, or by putting "both feet in or out" of their choice.

The $2 bill reminds us of our choice to be free, independent, and happy. The secret of happiness is in three choices. Any time you feel upset, angry, or trapped, there is something in your life that you are not accepting. The courage to make one of these three choices will give you back your freedom and peace of mind. The choices are as follows:

1. You can change your situation (relationship or work) which takes courage as you face and conquer your fears. For example, if someone is always judgmental or critical of you and this is a deal breaker, then you can tell them that behavior is no longer acceptable to you, and if they continue you will leave the relationship. If they stop this unacceptable behavior, then you will stay and be at peace. If not, you choose number two.

2. You can leave the situation (i.e., relationship or work).

3. If you can't change the situation or you choose not to leave the situation then you can stay and accept the "what is" of the situation and be totally at peace with the situation because it is your choice.

Summary

Dr. Ace's financial freedom guide is very basic.

- First, write your new money story and set your goals for increasing your income, eliminating your debt first, and then increasing your savings and investments.

- Create a practice that you love, that is profitable, and then do more of it. Many dentist/owners that I coach complain about some of the people they work with who make them miserable. I tell them to go back to their office and tell the owner to fire those people. Then I remind them that *they are the owner*. Most people forget they can make their practice exactly what they want it to be. They have the canvas and the brush.

- Learn to make more money in your practice and focus that money toward debt reduction. Once you are debt-free, you can put your money in a safe, stress-free environment. Most doctors who are still working should create a Private Family Bank maximizing your contributions (https://smartestwealthsystems.com/PFB-for-dentists). With any excess money you can take advantage of 15% or greater drops in the market and invest on their own in a Schwab or Vanguard account in the United States market through index funds such as the S&P 500 or total US stock market, as I mentioned earlier. Once you feel comfortable investing on your own, share your knowledge and this book with other colleagues.

- Stop listening to the news and worrying about what's happening in the market. This is just noise. That's it. Now, enjoy your life, give gratitude and spend the rest of your money on things that add meaning to your life. This leads to financial freedom and a life of self-integrity and peace.

- Economic peace of mind is more than just financial freedom. In fact, we can experience economic peace of mind long before we reach financial freedom. *Once we have a solid guide in place for achieving financial freedom, we can let go of our anxiety about money and live as if it has already happened.* With this newfound peace of mind, we can truly enjoy life in the moment because we are secure in what we have, and we know that we can deal with any life challenge.

We can face life with joy and excitement once we have a vision and a beautiful story for our lives. With *this book*, each of us can claim both financial freedom *and* economic and personal peace of mind. "Being happy is a choice."

ACKNOWLEDGMENTS

To my wife, Nancy, who has always been supportive of my adventures and misadventures while creating an incredible life for myself and our children.

To my father, who showed me the problems with gambling and spending recklessly and died broke at age 65. To my mother, who understood getting out of debt early, saving and investing safely, and who retired a millionaire, living to be eighty-seven.

To my financial mentors,

Kendrick Mercer, my coauthor on my last book, who taught me "If you have it made, why risk it?"—but more importantly, taught me how to live my life in peace and contentment.

John Cummuta, who trained me on the importance of debt reduction.

Daniel R. Solin, who taught me the simplicity of just buying the S&P 500 index.

William Bernstein, whose down-to-earth investment books help me clarify my investment strategy through his humor and common-sense approach.

Warren Buffett, who has been an example of loving your work and living a great and simple life, and who taught me the importance of buying stocks on sale and keeping the investments forever.

Dr. Denny Southard, who taught me the power and value of dividend investing.

Ben Franklin, one of our nation's founding fathers, who exemplified living frugally until you are out of debt and creating prosperity through hard work and sound business principles. Franklin's book is titled *The Way to Wealth*.

To all those stupid financial mistakes I made as a dentist, which caused me great pain while teaching me important lessons I remember well enough to share with you now.

To my athletic coaches (Mr. Bill Granger, Mr. Dick Truman, and Mr. Ralph Maughan), who taught me the importance of compassion and commitment of time and energy required to help any person reach their highest potential.

To all my incredible clinical mentors (Drs. Jefferson Jones, Fred Seymour, Manny Wiseman, Joe Neaverth, Stephen Cohen, John McSpadden, Gary Carr, and Steve Buchanan), who saw the possibilities in a not-so-smart individual, allowing me to increase my clinical skills so I would have more satisfaction and fun in my profession over the years.

To my twenty-year Army experience, which helped mold my leadership skills and revealed to me the importance of empowering people.

To my dental team and especially my office manager, Melissa, who has made my time in the office fun and effortless.

To Dr. Arlen Lackey, who took me under his wing and trained me to present at the national level.

To all my practice management coaches (Linda Miles, Dr. Mike Abernathy, Greg Stanley and Wes Warren, Dr. Bill Blatchford), who helped me create a culture in my practice that was fun and profitable.

To Alex Nottingham, Drs. Jim Kulild, Hugh Habas and Doug Carlsen, who thoroughly reviewed my rough draft and gave me valuable insights and made important corrections.

To Cynthia Goerig, the CEO of Endo Mastery, and our head coach, Debra Miller, who have given me great insights into practice management and how to obtain incredible success and results for our clients.

To my publisher, John Koehler of Koehler Books, and their editors, who helped make this possible.

APPENDIX A

Resources from Dr. Ace

Alexander, Michael A. *Stock Cycles: Why Stocks Won't Beat Money Markets Over the Next Twenty Years*. Writers Club Press, 2000.

Bernstein, William J. *If You Can: How Millennials Can Get Rich Slowly*. William J. Bernstein, 2014.

Bernstein, William J. *The Four Pillars of Investing: Lessons for Building a Winning Portfolio Hardcover*. McGraw Hill, 2010.

Bernstein, William J. *The Investor's Manifesto: Preparing for Prosperity, Armageddon, and Everything in Between*. John Wiley and Sons, Hoboken, NJ, 2010.

Bogle, John C. *The Little Book of Common Sense Investing: The Only Way to Guarantee Your Fair Share of Stock Market Returns*. Wiley, Hoboken, NJ, 2017.

Chapman, Gary D. *The Five Love Languages: How to Express Heartfelt Commitment to Your Mate*. Thorndike Press, Waterville, ME, 2005.

Clason, George S. *The Richest Man in Babylon*. Dauphin Publications, 2017.

Clements, Jonathan. *The Little Book of Main Street Money: 21 Simple Truths That Help Real People Make Real Money*. LLC Gildan Media, 2009.

Clements, Jonathan. Website: https://humbledollar.com/money-guide/main-menu/

Cummuta, John M. *Turn Your Debt into Wealth: A Proven System for Real Financial Freedom*. Simon & Schuster Audio, 2001.

Cummuta, John M. *The Banker's Secret to Permanent Family Wealth: Live your life . . . And build your wealth . . . Using the same money*. The smartest wealth system, 2017.

Dahle, James M., MD. *The White Coat Investor: A Doctor's Guide to Personal Finance And Investing*. The White Coat Investor LLC, 2014.

Dahle, James M., MD. Website: https://www.whitecoatinvestor.com/

Goerig, Albert C., and Mercer, Kendrick. *Time and Money: Your Guide to Economic Freedom*. ACG Press, Olympia, WA, 2004.

Hyman, Mark. *Food: What the Heck Should I Eat?* Little, Brown and Company, 2018.

Hyman, Mark. *The Five Forces of Wellness: The Ultra Prevention System for Living an Active, Age-Defying, Disease-Free Life* Audio CD. 2006.

Headley, Jason. "It's Not About The Nail." YouTube. May 22, 2013. https://www.youtube.com/watch?v=-4EDhdAHrOg.

Malkiel, Burton Gordon, and Ellis, Charles D. *The Elements of Investing: Easy Lessons for Every Investor*. Wiley, Hoboken, NJ, 2013.

Malkiel, Burton Gordon. *A Random Walk Down Wall Street: The Time-tested Strategy for Successful Investing*. W.W. Norton & Company, New York, 2016.

Robbins, Anthony, and Mallouk, Peter. *Unshakeable: Your Financial Freedom Playbook*. New York: Simon & Schuster, 2017.

Sinek, Simon. *Start with Why: How Great Leaders Inspire Everyone to Take Action*. Penguin Group, New York, NY. Dec 27, 2011.

Sinek, Simon. *Leaders Eat Last: Why Some Teams Pull Together and Others Don't*. Penguin Group, New York, NY. May 23, 2017.

Solin, Daniel R. *The Smartest Investment Book You'll Ever Read: The Proven Way to Beat the "Pros" and Take Control of Your Financial Future*. Pedigree Books, New York, NY, 2010.

Solin, Daniel R. *The Smartest Money Book You'll Ever Read: Everything You Need to Know about Growing, Spending, and Enjoying Your Money*. Penguin Group, New York, NY 2011.

Solin, Daniel R. *The Smartest Retirement Book You'll Ever Read*. Penguin Group, New York, NY 2010.

Stanley, Thomas J. and Danko, William D. *Millionaire Next Door: The Surprising Secrets of America's Wealthy*. Taylor Trade Publishing, 2010.

Stanley, Thomas J. and Fallaw, Sarah Stanley. *The Next Millionaire*

Next Door: Enduring Strategies for Building Wealth. The Rowan and Littlefield Publishing Group, 2019.

Swedroe, Larry E., and Hempen, Joe H. *The Only Guide to a Winning Bond Strategy You'll Ever Need: The Way Smart Money Preserves Wealth Today.* Saint Martin's Press, New York, 2006.

Tobias, Andrew. *The Only Investment Guide You'll Ever Need.* Second Mariners books edition, New York, 2016.

Wattles, Wallace. *The Science of Getting Rich.* April, 1910.

Wright, Kelley. *Dividends Still Don't Lie: The Truth About Investing in Blue Chip Stocks and Winning in the Stock Market.* Wiley, Hoboken, NJ, 2010.

Zweig, Jason. *Your Money and Your Brain: How the New Science of Neuroeconomics Can Help Make You Rich.* Simon and Schuster, New York, NY, 2007.

APPENDIX B

Step-by-Step Debt Reduction Plan

Act Today. Declaring that you are seriously committed to getting out of debt is the first step in achieving personal wealth. Go through the steps below. All forms can be downloaded from DoctorAce.com.

1. Sit down with your significant other: Both of you must be on board, knowing that this will strengthen your relationship, eliminate stress around money and give you back your freedom. Then read this book together, and then set time aside to do the following.

2. Add up your net worth, that is, everything you own, and then subtract everything you owe in the chart on the next page.

DETERMINE YOUR NET WORTH			
ASSETS	AMOUNT	LIABILITIES	AMOUNT
Personal Cash (Bank)			
Practice Cash (Bank)			
Taxable Investments (stocks)			
Tax Deferred Investments (IRA/401K)			
Cash Value Life Insurance			
Gold/Silver			
Other			
Real Estate		How much is owed	
Main Home		How much is owed	
Vacation Homes		How much is owed	
Rental Property		How much is owed	
Practice Building		How much is owed	
Practice (value =2 times net)		How much is owed	
Other Assets		How much is owed	
Automobiles/ Boat		How much is owed	
Personal Property		How much is owed	

Pension (value = 20X yearly amt)		**School Loans**	
Social Security (value = 20X yearly amount)		**Credit cards debt**	
		Other debt	
Total assets $		**Total liabilities $**	
		Net worth $ (Assets-Liabilities)	

3. Write down your total household income.

Net income source (after taxes)	Earner A	Earner B
Salary (net, take-home pay)		
Part-time or self-employment income		
Home-based business income		
Investment income		
Social Security		

Pension		
Veteran's benefits		
Other		
Individual totals		
Total income of A and B		

4. Reducing your monthly expenses. List all your current monthly expenses in the "current" column below. In the "reduced" column, record the lowest amount you can reasonably spend on each item. Total up all "reduced" amounts at the bottom of column 3, then subtract that amount from your total income. The resulting number is your maximum possible starting your *found debt reduction money.* Go through your credit card receipts and checkbook and add up all your monthly expenses. Use the list below. See where you can eliminate or reduce certain expenses.

MONTHLY EXPENSES	CURRENT	REDUCED
Retirement plan contributions		
Going out for lunch at work		
Dining out (other than work lunches)		
Groceries (use coupons)		
Telephone (including cell phone)		
Heating fuel		
Water/sewer		
Electricity		
Car cost (fuel and maintenance)		
Parking, tolls, etc. (car pool or bus)		
Car #1 payment		
Car #2 payment		

Insurance—automobile (higher deductibles)		
Insurance—health (higher deductibles)		
Insurance—home (umbrella insurance)		
Insurance—life (buy only term)		
Insurance—other		
Home equity loan payment		
Re-finance home mortgage (walk away)		
Other loan payment		
Child care		
Cable or satellite TV		
Movies out		
DVD rental		
Other entertainment		

Sports (golf, fishing, etc.)		
Health club		
Lawn maintenance		
Laundry and dry cleaning		
Pet food and care		
Subscriptions		
Online computer services		
Credit card payment		
Credit card payment		
Credit card payment		
Christmas gifts		
College education for children		
Private schools		

Emergency fund		
Other savings		
Total reduced monthly expenses =		

**Total income—reduced monthly expenses =
(this is your *found debt reduction money* used to
accelerate your debt payments)**

5. Other ideas to find extra money.

- Stop funding retirement until debt-free, except for matching contributions.
- Get rid of your emergency fund. Once your credit card is paid, it becomes your emergency fund.
- Evaluate/reduce holiday gift giving.
- Check bank/credit card statement.
- Stop smoking.
- Properly maintain your home and car.
- Never buy a brand-new car until debt-free.
- Never finance beyond 36 months.
- Take advantage of "cheap," meaningful vacations.
- Don't buy tools/boats you don't use a lot—rent them instead.
- Conserve utility usage.
- Avoid "Retail Therapy."
- Learn to say "No" to kids.
- Stop funding for children's education. Let them pay for their own college.
- All bonuses and pay raises go towards paying down debt.

- Eliminate private mortgage insurance (PMI) by paying down the mortgage balance to 80% of the home's original appraised value.
- Evaluate your real insurance needs.
- Auto insurance (get higher deductibles)
- Personal liability insurance
- Medical insurance
- Get higher deductibles.
- Get an umbrella attachment.
- Never buy extended warranties.
- Use coupons (retailmenot.com, gethoney.com).
- Stop getting tax refunds.
- Spare change jar
- Have only a cell phone.
- Minimize dining out, and make brown bag lunches.
- Simplify your lifestyle.
- Entertainment
- Movies
- Get rid of cable
- Shop at outlet malls/Goodwill/consignment shops
- See if you can refinance your home through Quicken Loans or a local bank.

The following ideas are for your office team members who want to get out of debt. You just need to learn how to be more efficient and be more profitable in your own practice.
An extra job becomes the rocket booster to accelerate your debt reduction.

- Make more at your job and put it toward debt.
- Do consulting work from home.
- Set up an eBay business at home.

- Visit clients at their home (bookkeepers or computer experts).
- Teach college at night.
- Check out the internet for "work-at-home jobs" (watch out for scams).
- Investigate doing multilevel marketing (Mary Kay) and watch out for scams.
- With an extra job, you could be debt-free three years faster.
  6. Develop a spending journal and for a month: write down each purchase you make (except regularly scheduled bills). This includes incidentals such as coffee, parking and other items less than a dollar. Use mint.com or download from DoctorAce.com.

Date	Item purchased	Cash	Credit	Check	Amount

  7. Use the snowball approach (described below) to pay off all debts within seven to ten years. Read through the snowball approach description, and then fill out the debt form to see how long it will take you to pay off all debts by making a 10% or 20% payment toward debt each month. I am not a big fan

of budgeting. If you are serious about getting out of debt, automatically take 10% or 20% out of your bank account each month as if it were a tax. Live on the rest. **Automation of the payments is the secret!** Filling out the below form will help you understand your financial goals.

SNOWBALL WORKSHEET

Identify your debts and record them on the Snowball Worksheet below (you can go to Doctorace.com and download the worksheet). First, pay all small debts (under $10,000) starting with the smallest. This "small debt" category includes credit card debt, consumer debt, auto loan balances, and small student loans. Start with the smallest debt (no matter how high or low the interest) and then use the money from your *debt reduction savings account* to pay it off first, while continuing to make the minimum payments on your other debts.

At the beginning, it's important to get momentum and see that you are making progress, so don't worry about the respective interest rates now. If the high credit card interest rate on a larger debt bothers you, you can always call the company and successfully negotiate a lower rate or transfer your balance to another credit card company with a lower rate.

Once you have paid off the first debt, you'll feel a sense of empowerment. Paying off that debt frees up additional money, which you add to your savings. Use this increased savings to pay down the next-smallest debt. Fill out the worksheet in pencil so that you can update it each month. This will help you keep on track and stay motivated.

As you pay down debt, you gain momentum and free up more money to pay off the next debt. The money that pays off these debts comes from increased income, reduced spending, and the extra money that becomes available as you pay off each debt. If you have money saved when you begin setting in motion *Dr. Ace's Financial Freedom Guide*, for the sake of your peace of mind, do *not* use that money for early debt reduction for at least six months. Below is an example of how we snowball paying off debt.

First, determine what percentage of income you want to pay toward debt. If you and your spouse's average income is $72,000, you would divide this by 12 months, giving you $6,000; after taxes that would be $5,000. Ten percentage of this would be $500 per month.

The $500 (10%) will be paid each month to the principal of the top loan in the chart. First, add the $500 to the Visa card $30 payment, giving you $530 per month to pay toward that loan, which will be paid off in two months. When the Visa card is paid off, apply that $530 plus $32 to the next MasterCard loan, which will result in $562; it will take three months to pay off *that* loan. Your efforts will continue to snowball throughout all your debt. The debts will be paid off in seven years and four months and you will have an extra $31,176 per year to invest, save, take vacations, send children through college, or work less.

$500 (10%) Paid Monthly to Principal of Top Loan in the Chart

Name of Debt	Total Balance (smallest to largest)	Monthly Payment	Accelerated Monthly Payment	Months to pay off
Visa Card	$1,000	$30	$530	2
MasterCard	$1,500	$32	$562	3
Department Store	$2,000	$36	$598	4
Car 1	$9,200	$520	$1,118	9
Car 2	$14,300	$750	$1,868	8

Home Equity Loan	$26,000	$370	$2,238	12
Mortgage at 4.5%	$155,000	$860	$3,098	50
Totals	$209,000	$2,598 ($31,176/yr.)		88 months (7yrs. 4mo.)

$1,000 (20%) Paid Monthly to Principal of Top Loan in the Chart

Name of Debt	Total Balance (smallest to largest)	Monthly Payment	Accelerated Monthly Payment	Months to pay off
Visa Card	$1,000	$30	$1,030	1
MasterCard	$1,500	$32	$1,062	2
Department Store	$2,000	$36	$1,098	2
Car 1	$9,200	$520	$1,618	6
Car 2	$14,300	$750	$2,368	6
Home Equity Loan	$26,000	$370	$2,738	10
Mortgage at 4.5%	$155,000	$860	$3,098	43
Totals	$209,000	$2,598 ($31,176/yr.)		70 months (5yrs. 7mo.)

YOUR SNOWBALL WORKSHEET: CALCULATE PAYING OFF YOUR DEBT

(Annual household income: $)

(Average American debt is 2.5 times the annual household income)

1. **Determine your extra monthly payments: $**

 Try for 10% or more of your monthly take-home income. If you only have a home mortgage, then you should add 20% to 30% of your monthly take-home income to your mortgage payment.

2. **Write down each debt in the first column below**, prioritizing each debt from smallest to largest. Again, do not be overly concerned about the interest rate.

3. **Using the snowball approach, add your accelerator margin to the smallest debt** by making this new monthly payment. Put this in column 4. To determine when the debt will be paid off, divide this amount into the total balance of that debt by the new monthly payment in column 4, and put the number of months to pay off in column 5.

4. **When this debt is paid off, add what used to be the monthly payment amount to the next smallest debt** payment and place that in column 4. Again, divide this amount into the total balance of that debt by your new monthly payment in column 4. Put the number of months to pay off in column 5.

5. **Continue adding each paid-off debt's monthly payment amount to its accelerated monthly payment** and rolling the total amount to the next debt.

6. **Add up the months in column 5 to determine when all debts will be paid off.**

Name of Debt	Total Balance	Monthly Payment	Accelerated Monthly Payment	Months to Pay Off
1	2	3	4	5
Totals				

Things to keep in mind about your debt-elimination plan:

- Use only minimum payments to maximize the debt elimination process.
- Use only the principal and interest portion of your mortgage payment for purpose of calculation (not tax/insurance).
- Interest rates are not a big factor.
- Only non-recurring debts go into your debt-elimination plan.

8. Write and post your Financial Goals. For instance, "I am taking 10% of my income and paying off my debts. In six months (date), I will use 20% of my income toward an extra payment on my debts. I will pay off all credit card debts in one year (date), my car in two years (date), and my home in six years (date)." Then each month, review and challenge yourself to increase your debt reduction.

9. Develop a support group of either family or co-workers. In most families, issues of money cause the greatest stress and most do not understand how debt can keep a person in prison and take two-thirds of their income throughout their lifetime. In my office, I created and presented to them and their spouse a debt reduction plan which you will find at DoctorAce.com. In this program I showed them how to pay off debt, including their home, within ten years—thereby freeing up more money to invest in their retirement fund. I also showed them how to invest safely with little risk and higher returns. (Remember Lisa's story in Chapter 2.)

10. Sign up for Dave Ramsey's financial peace University. Sometimes it helps go to a program where there is some accountability, and this is one of the better programs and is available everywhere. Http://www.daveramsey.com/fpu/

11. Continue to read books such as found in this book's references, and listen to audios about debt reduction, including the ones found at DoctoerAce.com.

12. Celebrate success.

This is NOT a *no-spending* plan; it is a *managed-spending* plan. I am not saying you shouldn't spend any money on the things you want, but I DO want you to be aware of the impact that each expenditure has on your ability to build your wealth. Most people can easily spend and live on half the amount they normally spend.

APPENDIX C

The Ten Principles of Investment and Debt

By following these Ten Principles, you can achieve financial freedom:

1. The key to financial freedom is to make more than you spend or spend less than you make.

2. Make sure that every asset, large and small, adds meaning to your life.

3. Your best source of money is your ability to earn it, not investing.

4. If you have it made, don't risk it. You now can save enough money to retire early if you just play it smart by putting your money in safe investments as described in Chapter 5.

5. Because your source of money is your ability to earn it, rather than investment returns, focus on ways to increase your income: make yourself more valuable

at your job, go back to school or work part-time until you become debt-free.

6. No matter how much you make, always automatically take 10% to 20% and pay off your debts. Spend less than you make or make more than you spend.

7. Only keep material possessions that add meaning to your life and get rid of the rest: it is just junk.

8. Insurance *is not an investment,* according to these principles. Its only purpose is to replace money in the case of an unexpected loss, such as disability or death; keep it to the minimum necessary. Once you reach financial freedom, it becomes an unnecessary expenditure.

9. Purchasing a home is an effective use of debt. Although it is not a liquid asset, it adds meaning to your life. Homes have also proven to be good long-term investments and provide a hedge against inflation.

10. Always save for consumption; never borrow for consumer items, vacations, and so forth. Pay off all credit cards and consumer debt in full each month.

APPENDIX D

Understand Investing and How the Markets Work

Daniel Solin has written many must-read investment books. In two of these books, *The Smartest Money Book You'll Ever Read* and *The Smartest Investment Book You'll Ever Read,* he summarized the key points about investing:

- It is not complicated.

- No one has a clue where the market is headed.

- Stay away from individual stocks that expose you to higher risk without higher expected returns.

- Stay away from actively managed mutual funds (brokers) that increase your fees, cost, and reduce your expected return.

- Never use the services of a broker or advisor who claims to be able to beat the market.

- Determine your asset allocation and invest in low-cost index funds such as the Schwab S&P 500 (passively managed) index fund, which will beat 96% of all financial advisors and brokers. There are other more conservative investments listed below.

- The free market system works. Stocks prices are random and efficient. There is no mispricing. Always stay in the market.

- Don't listen to the news (turn off the noise).

UNDERSTANDING THE RISKS OF THE MARKET

Very few people understand the stock market, and no one can accurately predict changes in the market. Jack Bogle, the founder of Vanguard group, says, "Nobody knows nothing about the market." Many brokers tell you to buy a stock when it is high and tell you not to buy when it drops. But common sense would tell us the best time to buy stocks is when they're low. Even worse, some brokers tell you to get out of the market when it drops. When we invest in equities (stocks) we are always on shifting sands; we are always taking a risk. And when we invest, we should not invest in actively managed mutual funds, but stay with low-cost passively managed index funds such as the S&P 500, which has consistently done better than 96% of all funds on the market.

When you have a guide to obtain financial freedom that is safe and predictable, why take a risk? Anyone who can work and save money has it made; financial freedom is yours for the taking. Your ability to earn money and pay off debt is the most important thing in developing economic abundance. Your income is like a large inflation-protected bond that allows you to put a greater amount of your investment portfolio into stocks. Investments are for your retirement and your peace of mind, not to make you rich. Your earnings from your job will make you rich if you live within your means and consistently save or store part of them. Dentists who do this now work two to three days a week and continue to do something they really enjoy that brings in money. They will never, ever use up the money they've set aside for retirement.

THE BIG SCAM

According to *Forbes* ("Why the Average Investor's Return Is So Low," by Sean Hanlon, April 24, 2014), over a ten-year period (2004 to 2013), the S&P 500 has averaged 7.4% return. The reason average investors have only realized a 2.6% return during that same time is because they are in actively managed funds which constantly trade in and out of the market, and the investors pay high fees in commissions, trading fees and taxes to their brokers. Many brokers buy and sell securities within the funds repeatedly, to try to improve their performance. This boosts transaction cost and taxes. These costs are buried in your management fees which compensate the fund manager. These can cost you up to 3% to 4% annually. Many fund managers keep money in cash, so they can time the market. This is called *cash drag* and gives you a zero performance on that money, compared with what you could've gotten in an index fund.

Most individual investors rely upon money managers, advisers and brokers who engage in hyperactive trading to try to beat the market by picking winners and timing the market. This is a losing strategy. In most cases, investors would be better off consistently investing in index funds like the S&P 500. Jack Bogle, founder of the Vanguard group, believes in index funds and says actively managed funds are a big scam. When you invest in loaded actively managed mutual funds, you put up 100% of the capital and take 100% of the risk, and if you make money, they take up to 70% or more of the upside in fees. And if you lose money, they still get paid. They are charging you ten to 30 times what it would cost for you to buy a low-cost index fund which would match the market and beat 96% of the mutual funds. Because fees are the enemy of the individual investor, we need to stay away from financial advisors and brokers who work on commission and thus put us into actively managed funds.

Here is an example from one of my clients who had over $1.6 million that was managed by a large brokerage firm. Over a six-year period, his portfolio would have built *$863,881 more in assets* if it had been placed into a Schwab S&P 500 fund. Compare your portfolio to the S&P 500 and see how you do. Go to DebtFreeDentist.com for more videos and audios and download and fill out the Excel comparison sheet seen below.

Remember, the S&P 500 fund performs better than 96% of all other managed funds, and I have yet to see any of my clients whose portfolio has done better than the S&P 500 index fund. In most cases, they have lost significant amounts of money when they let the experts invest for them.

	Schwab S&P 500 mutual fund index annual return	Brokerage **trust** account	annual % return	**Loss**	Brokerage **401K** account	annual % return	**Loss**
Ticker sym	SWPPX						
Fees	0.03%		1%				
Cost/ 1M$	$300		$10,000				
Stocks/Bonds	100%/0		100%/0				
Invested		Opening balance			Opening balance		
2017	21.80%	$406,560	12.00%	($39,843)	$1,276,633	9.50%	($157,026)
2016	12.0%	$321,784	6.5%	($17,698)	$1,099,332	1.27%	($117,958)
2015	1.4%	$316,367	-2.3%	($11,706)	$1,262,352	-2.28%	($46,455)
2014	13.7%	$302,687	4.5%	($27,847)	$1,322,966	6.29%	($98,032)
2013	32.4%	$356,161	7.9%	($87,259)	$1,186,118	11.37%	($249,441)
2012	16.0%	$272,222	12.1%	($10,617)		Loss	($668,911)
			Loss	($194,970)			
						Total Loss	($863,881)

	Schwab S&P 500 mutual fund index	Brokerage taxable account Opening balance each year	Added money that year	Total invested	Your brokarage return that year	Loss (red) Gain (black)
Ticker sym	SWPPX					
Fees	0.03%				1%	
Cost/ 1M$	$300				$10,000	
Stocks/Bonds	100%/0				100%/0	
Invested		Opening balance	Added money			
2018	-4.40%			$0	#DIV/0!	#DIV/0!
2017	21.80%			$0	#DIV/0!	#DIV/0!
2016	12.0%			$0	#DIV/0!	#DIV/0!
2015	1.4%			$0	#DIV/0!	#DIV/0!
2014	13.7%			$0	#DIV/0!	#DIV/0!
2013	32.4%			$0	#DIV/0!	#DIV/0!
2012	16.0%			$0	#DIV/0!	#DIV/0!
2011	2.1%			$0	#DIV/0!	#DIV/0!
2010	15%			$0	#DIV/0!	#DIV/0!
2009	26.30%			$0	#DIV/0!	#DIV/0!
					Total Loss/gain	#DIV/0!

Another must-read book is Anthony Robbins' *Unshakeable*. He writes about the two enemies of the investor: fear and fees. Most money is lost in the market because of these two factors. If you are an investor and put your money in an actively managed mutual fund, you will pay 3.17% of the non-taxable account toward fees (4.17% if it's a taxable account). Look at the chart below to see what this 3% difference in fees would cost you over 20, 30, or 40 years if the S&P 500 average 7% growth. You would have two to three times more earnings.

	4% growth	7% growth	Earnings Difference
30 years	$191,996	$425,948	2.2x
30 years	$504,544	$1,300,631	2.6x
40 years	$1,058,851	$3,220,187	3.1x

The second greatest enemy of the investor is fear. Getting out of the market when it starts to drop is a mistake. This is the time you need to *buy*. You have a good portfolio of index funds you should always stay in, because they will always rebound. From 1997 to 2016, the S&P 500 index returned 7.7%. If you were out of the market during the top ten days, your return would've dropped to 4%; the top 20 days, your return would've been 1.6%; and if you were out of the market the top 40 days, your return would've been a *negative* 2.4%. The message is clear: when the market drops, *do not* get out of the market, and continually keep buying more index funds like the S&P 500 as it drops. The free market system works. Stock prices are random and efficient. There is no mispricing. Always stay in the market.

UNDERSTANDING INDEX FUNDS

Many *individual* stocks are not safe on a long-term basis, which is why we focus on *index funds* that represent the whole United States market and thus spread the risk across many securities. Warren Buffett, the legendary investor and business magnate, believes in the American economy, and has said that he would invest the money he leaves to his children in a Vanguard S&P 500 fund. An index fund is a passively managed mutual fund made up of the securities (stocks or bonds) in a stock index in the proportions the index devises. The most famous stock market indexes are the Dow Jones industrial average (DJIA) and the Standard and Poor's 500 (S&P 500). The DJIA is based on 30 major companies; the S&P 500 has 500 companies; the QQQ (NASDAQ) has 4,000 companies; and the Wilshire 5000 total market index is the broadest index for the US stock market.

The advantages of investing in index funds are as follows:

- Passive investing (avoids excessive fees, commissions and taxes)
- Diversification spreads risk across many securities.
- Low management fees
- Income from dividend returns
- Predictable risk (lower than individual securities)
- Easy to purchase
- Performance better than 96% of actively managed funds

ACTIVELY MANAGED FUNDS COMPARED TO INDEX (PASSIVELY MANAGED) FUNDS

In actively managed funds, the financial advisor or broker tries to beat the market by timing the market and selecting stocks. This results in the client's money moving into and out of the market numerous times and leads to a high commission for the financial advisor and expenses to the investor through trading costs, short-term capital gains tax, and cash drag (money held out of the market and not being invested). These expenses significantly reduce your overall return, and most of these funds never beat the average S&P 500 index fund. This 3% to 4% expense result in a 50% to 70% loss in the return of your investments over time. This is why fees are so important. You can get an S&P 500 index fund for as little as 0.03% (three basis points), which mirrors the components of a market index and has no other costs.

CORRECTIONS IN THE MARKET

There are always corrections in the market and you must welcome them with excitement rather than fear. This is a great opportunity to buy more index funds on sale. At the bottom of the bear market in October 1974, Forbes interviewed Buffett and asked him how he felt. He said, *"Like an oversexed guy in a whorehouse, there are so many choices. Now is the time to invest and get rich."* This is a paradigm shift and we must develop an attitude of excitement, not fear, when the market drops, because that's when stocks are on sale. Below is a chart of the average historical corrections of the market from 1900 to 2015.

Average Historical Corrections of the Market				
	Regular Decline (5% or more)	Modest Correction (10% or more)	Serious Correction (15% or more	Bear Market (20% or more)
Frequency	3 times/ year	1 times/year	Every 2 years	Every 3 years
Average loss before drop ends	11%	19%	27%	35%
Average duration	40 days	109 days	217 days	364 days

In his recent book, *Unshakeable*, Tony Robbins states that over the past 70 years, there have only been 14 bear markets averaging one every five years and lasting an average of one year and ranging from 45 days to nearly two years. He says that what you need to know is that bear markets don't last and are always followed by a bull market during the next 12 months. From March 9, 2009, the S&P 500 index surged by 69.5% over the next 12 months.

Since 2009 we have not had a bear market (20 % or more drop) and only one 17% drop in 2010 and an 18% drop in 2011. Since then we have had only ten corrections in the S&P 500 that were greater than 10%. 2018 was a very volatile year with a 7%, 11% and 19.7%. This is probably because of the ending of the Federal Reserve's policy of quantitative easing from 2009 to 2014 and low interest rates, forcing more investors into the market. 2018 was a great year to test your risk tolerance and an excellent year to buy stocks at the bottom. Even though there were significant corrections, the overall loss that year was a -4.4%. Remember, it only becomes a loss if you sell.

Remember that the market is just a place to store your money for better long-term returns while you routinely and automatically invest each month through dollar-cost averaging (DCA) which takes advantage of market corrections. Long-term investing in stocks like the S&P 500 can give you 3 to 4 times the return, compared to a less-risky bond portfolio. When you are debt-free, it becomes easier to invest into stocks like the S&P 500. For most investors, this is all we need to do and we can quit worrying about the market.

DEALING WITH YOUR INVESTMENT EMOTIONS

As humans we are wired with a fight-or-flight emotional base. Our emotions make life worth living but uncontrolled emotions while investing can be deadly. I highly recommend that you read Jason Zweig's book entitled *Your Money and Your Brain: How the New Science of Neuroeconomics Can Help Make You Rich*— it will help you understand your emotions during investing. If you are unable to understand or cannot discipline and control your emotions when there is a 10%, 20% or even 40% drop in the market, then you should stay in liquid assets such as short-term bonds and accept your mediocre returns. Great investors spend little time watching the market but do have a simple and safe game plan that they stick with. They have patience, available cash, courage, and know market history well enough to wait for the drops in the market that always come. Once you understand the history of the market, then you respond with logic instead of a knee-jerk reaction from your fear. Stop listening to the financial (all) news throughout the year. Continue to contribute monthly, automatically, to the S&P 500 or US total stock market index fund in your Schwab account through dollar-cost averaging (DCA). When there is a greater than 10% drop in the market, buy more using your discretionary income. That's it, you're done. Keep it simple.

WHAT DO YOU DO WHEN THE MARKET TANKS?

When the stock market drops and we see our portfolio being reduced, our fight-or-flight emotions are stimulated. Long-term investors get excited rather than depressed because they realize the opportunities they have been given by this drop. Below is a step-by-step approach for you to remember during downturns in the market.

1. Understand and control your emotions. You need to switch your emotions to excitement because you are now able use your built-up cash in your money market account to buy the S&P 500 or dividend-paying stocks *on sale*. Warren Buffett says that opportunities of a 15% to 30% bear market drop rarely occur, and when they do, you need to buy as much of the good companies or S&P 500 as you can while they are on sale.

2. Remember that you have seen this picture before and you know how it ends, so **never sell** when the market drops.

3. Warren Buffett said if you can detach yourself from the crowd and become greedy while others are fearful, you can become very rich and you don't have to be smart. It does not take brains; it takes temperament.

4. Remind yourself that you are debt-free, have a constant source of income and that these great opportunities occur only a few times in your life.

5. Start rounding up more cash and hope it drops further for even greater opportunities.

6. Wonder what Warren Buffett is thinking (he is very happy).

7. As markets drop, your dividends will go up with your good dividend-paying Blue-Chip stocks.

8. As markets drop, your dividends will go up with your good dividend-paying Blue-Chip stocks.

9. Get back to loving your life.

Never try to time the market. The above technique is not about timing the market, but it is about taking advantage of the corrections the market especially those drops that are greater than 15%. This is what Warren Buffett does when he describes waiting for the best pitch before he swings and buying stocks on sale.

Stop listening to all the financial advice on television. This is just noise. Once you are debt-free and have a highly profitable, effortless and fun practice, you never have to worry about money again. Investing in index funds is the most efficient way to save your money and become rich slowly. You do not care about the market. Warren Buffett said if the stock market closed down for five years, it would not make a difference in his decision to invest. When you are debt-free, you will have abundant funds to invest in a safe and consistent manner and soon become financially free. Remember to always stay in the market and understand that drops in the market are opportunities to buy.

STEPS TO INDIVIDUAL INVESTING

When you learn to invest on your own you become the chess player not the chess piece. With the internet, investing in the market is very simple. You first need to open a brokerage account with a well-known investment company that provides excellent service with low fees and a wide range of low-cost index funds. I believe that both Vanguard and Schwab are excellent companies. **So, do it** *today*. I work with both but mostly with Schwab because it is open 24 hours a day, seven days a week and has excellent representatives and brokers. Schwab also requires no dollar minimums to open an account, the lowest expense ratios, and when you buy its mutual funds and index ETFs (exchange-traded funds), there are no trading costs, compared to other companies. All other trades are only $4.95 a trade.

Remember that all representatives and brokers from Schwab and Vanguard are salaried; they do not work on commission, so their advice focuses on your best interests. The company also has agents located in most cities. These local brokers can help you through the process, or you may go online and have an account set up within 30 minutes. Once you set up an account, then you can start putting money into specific mutual funds or follow some of the strategies that I will mention below. I also recommend becoming familiar with the Yahoo Finance and Morningstar websites to help you best understand the past performance of different funds.

INVESTMENT STRATEGIES

If you follow this guide, get out of debt and create a fun and profitable practice, you will never have to worry about money. Most dentists could be totally debt-free in seven to ten years. With a good practice management consultant, it could be three to six years. Just don't do stupid things with money. Get out of debt, improve your profitability and invest safely without fees as described in this book. Now, stop worrying. Below are five investment options outlined to put your mind at ease knowing you are getting the best return on your investments within your risk tolerance without paying high fees and commissions. *You can pick one or two of these options and you're done. It's that simple*. They run themselves and you never worry about getting out of the market. These models are based on my experiences and other investment books I have read, especially those by Daniel R. Solin, William Bernstein and Jonathan Clements (Appendix A).

The best investment strategies are always simple and easy to understand. Brokers want to sell you complex investments that you don't understand so they can charge high fees and commissions which often results in lower returns to you as the investor. Once you understand your risk tolerance and how the market works over time, then select the options that fit your comfort zone and your desired rate of return. Remind yourself that you are a long-term investor, and then stay in the market during corrections. When the market drops, you should be elated because stocks are on sale, and this is the time to buy and add to your portfolio. But before you invest, you should first understand your asset allocation and risk tolerance.

ASSET ALLOCATION AND RISK TOLERANCE

There are two categories of investments. One is debt investments (which I will refer to as *bonds*), where you are the lender and get a stated rate of return, such as in US government treasuries (bonds, notes, and bills), government agency bonds, bank certificates of deposit (CDs), money market accounts, and municipal bonds. The other category is *equities*, which include stocks/mutual funds/ETFs, real estate, and precious metals. As an owner of equities (which I will refer to as *stocks*) you make money through dividends and appreciation of the equity.

When you invest in stocks, you choose greater risk and volatility than with debt-types of investments. Over the long term, stock index funds have always performed significantly better than bonds. Bonds do offer safety and lower returns, but the problem today is the low interest rate and low return on the short-term treasury bills that are available to you—possibly a 2% return. If you are risk-averse and cannot take a 10% to 20% drop in the market, then your best investment is in your own Private Family Bank using a specialized whole life insurance policy where you are guaranteed 5% tax-free return without any of the worries of market fluctuations. See below.

William Bernstein in his book, *"The Investors Manifesto,"* describes a simple way of determining your risk tolerance. He says, "When the market drops 10% to 20%, did the investor (a) sell, (b) hold steady, (c) buy more or (d) buy more and hope for even further declines to continue the process? The answers to this risk tolerance question are then, (a) low, (b) moderate, (c) high, and (d) very high. To be a successful investor and sleep well at night, you need to understand market history and be able to discipline your emotions.

Vanguard Portfolio Allocation Models (Historical Returns 1926—2018)						
	Income (low risk)			Balanced (medium risk)		
Stock%/ Bond%	0/100	20/80	30/70	40/60	50/50	60/40
Average return	5.4%	6.7%	7.3%	7.8%	8.4%	8.8%
Worst year loss	-8.1%	-10%	-14.2%	-18.4%	-22.5%	-26.6%
Best year gain	32.6%	29.8%	28.4%	27.9%	32.3%	36.7%
$1000 / month for 30 years	$902K	$1.16M	$1.28M	$1.44M	$1.63M	$1.77M

Vanguard Portfolio Allocation Models (Historical Returns 1926—2018) continued			
	Growth (high risk)		
Stock%/ Bond%	70/30	80/20	100/0
Average return	9.3%	9.6%	10.3%
Worst year loss	-30.7%	-34.9%	-43.1%
Best year gain	41.1%	45.4%	54.2%
$1000 / month for 30 years	$1.97M	$2.1M	$2.43M

INVESTMENT STRATEGIES NEED TO CHANGE WITH THE TIMES

The way we invest today is dramatically different than it was forty years ago. We can now go online, open a brokerage account with Schwab or Vanguard and buy low-cost index funds that match the market, and do better than 96% of all actively managed funds. In 1980, mortgage interest rates reached an all-time high of 18.4% and you could buy a 14%, non-callable, 30-year, AAA-rated, tax-free municipal bond. That was when you would only buy bonds. In early 2000, you could buy ten-year, AAA-rated, tax-free municipal bonds at 5% or 6% with a guaranteed after-tax yield of 8% to 9%. Back then, there was no need to risk your money in the stock market.

Over the past 15 years, interest rates have decreased to almost 0%. A ten-year treasury note or CD is only getting about 2.5% return, and this does not even keep up with inflation. This is a tragedy for those who are retired and living on a fixed income and relying on the interest from their investments. Fifteen years ago, they were getting around 5 % return in their bank saving accounts, and now they are getting less than 1%. If you are relying upon the interest from bonds to live on in your retirement, you may run out of money and may have to add more stock index funds to your portfolio.

Schwab and Vanguard have created index funds that help you diversify into various percentages of US and international stocks and bonds. These are the target market funds and Vanguard life strategy funds (see options 3a and 3b, below). The more averse you are to risk, the more of your portfolio should be in bonds. Over the ten years total US bond ETF's rates have dropped and have averaged a 2% over the past three years. The total international ETF's have done poorly and have averaged around 6.6% over the past ten years while the US total stock index funds have given high long-term returns were around 13% over the past ten years (see below).

	Vanguard S&P 500 mutual fund	Schwab S&P 500 index mutual fund	Schwab Total US Stock mutual fund	Vanguard Total US Stock ETF	Vanguard International stock index ETF	Schwab International stock index ETF	Vanguard total US bonds ETF	Schwab total US bonds ETF
Schwab and Vanguard Index Funds Return Comparisons 1/1/2019 (From Morningstar.com)								
Ticker symbol	VFIAX	SWPPX	SWTSX	VTI	VTIAX	SCHF	VBTLX	SCHZ
Expense ratio	0.04%	0.03%	0.03%	0.04%	0.11%	0.04%	0.06%	0.04%
Stocks/Bonds	100%/0	100%/0	100%/0	100%/0	100%/0	100%/0	0/100%	0/100%
1 year	-4.3%	-4.4%	-5.3%	-5.2%	-14.4%	-14.3%	-0.03%	-0.03%
3 years	9.2%	9.2%	8.9%	9.0%	4.5%	3.6%	2.0%	1.88%
5 years	8.5%	8.4%	7.8%	7.9%	0.9%	0.5%	2.5%	2.45%
10 years	13.1%	13.0%	13.2%	13.3%	6.6%		3.4%	
		S&P 500			International stocks		Bond ETF's	
$ return of $50k/year using the 10-year percentages	10-year	$1,032,001			$713,574		$600,368	
	20-year	$4,777,155			$2,083,649		$1,437,598	
	30-year	$19,423,499			$4,729,671		$2,623,295	

When you are buying stock index funds, you are buying United States businesses that, over time, will return three to four times what bond funds will earn. Many of these US businesses do have international holdings. You must see stock index funds investments as a savings account and stay in for the long term. Stock index funds are less risky the longer you hold them, while the longer the maturity of bonds, the riskier they become. But if you are one who gets upset with price fluctuations in the stock market, then you should not own stocks. Put your money into high-yielding bank CDs, Schwab money market accounts or short-term two- to five-year US treasury bonds.

Remember, even if we get a 10% return with our stock (S&P 500) portfolio, your real return would be about 7% once adjusted to 3% inflation. A portfolio of 50 % stocks and 50 % bonds only has an expected return of 6% and after adjusting for inflation of 3% you are now down to a return of 3%. That is why we need to eliminate the 1% fee you pay your advisor and the 2% fee for the mutual fund, which could leave us with 0% return. If you invested in bonds returning only about 2%, you would have a negative return. Because of the current historical low interest rates, bonds only return about 2%.

REMEMBER YOUR HISTORY

Warren Buffett likes to quote Mark Twain when he supposedly said, "History doesn't repeat itself, but it often rhymes." Michael Alexander wrote a book entitled *Stock Cycles*. He reviews the markets over 200 years of American history until the year 2000. During that time, we have had seven long-term bear and seven long-term bull markets. The total average real return in a long-term bull market was 13.2% while the average return in a long-term bear market was 0.3%. For example, from 1966 to 1982, the total real return was a -1.5%. But from 1982 to the year 2000 the average total real return of the market was 14.8%. Alexander then went on to predict that starting in 2000 there would be a long-term bear market. In March 2013, the price of the Standard & Poor's (S&P) 500 was 1527, the same price as it was in March 2000, resulting in no growth of the stock, which is why those 13 years are called the lost decade. Also, that time period was a very turbulent time for investors but an exceptionally great time for those understood the phrase by Warren Buffett who once said that as an investor, it is wise to *"be fearful when others are greedy and greedy when others are fearful."* Today many investors that think the market is reaching its peak, which may be one reason why Warren Buffett as of August 2018 has over $111 billion in cash equivalents. It has been over ten years since we have had a bear market and, like Warren, I am keeping some of my powder dry. After funding my Private Family Bank I will automatically put money into my Schwab account monthly keeping more money in liquid assets such as US treasuries and money market accounts that are returning over 2%. This is so I can take advantage of possible opportunities that could occur over the next one to three years. Remember, no one can predict the market, so on this matter you must make your own decision.

INVESTMENT OPTION BASED ON RISK

OPTION 1: SAFE—NO RISK—HIGHEST RETURN!!!

Pay off all debt which is mandatory *before* investing. Paying off debt is like getting the highest-grade inflation-protected bond with a guaranteed interest rate of over 100%, risk-free. Set up an automatic payment each month toward the principle of the next debt of your snowball payments.

Now that you are debt-free, it's a chance to create a systematic and consistent investment game plan. You will secure your financial freedom if you follow the total guide that is found in this book. This system gives you financial peace of mind and you never have to worry about what the market is doing. Remember to always stay in the market and never sell. Work with a representative from Charles Schwab or a Vanguard representative to set up your account.

Option 1b: Safe - No Risk—Tax-Free Return!

This option is for those who are fearful of the risks and ups and downs of the stock market and want a guaranteed return that grows in a safe tax-deferred environmnet. The Private Family Bank is created with a specifically designed whole life insurance policy available only through "mutually owned" life insurance companies. These policies are structured to reduce agents commissioned by 50% to 70% because it's designed to maximize your cash accumulation rather than your death benefit. Every dollar you use to eliminate your debts remain in your bank accumulating interest and dividends at the same time it's paying off your debts. At the end of the process, your debts are paid off and all the dollars you used to do it with are still in your bank, continually growing. The Private Family Bank should be maximized before investing in the market because it has the following advantages.

- It is one of the safest investments where all growth is tax free and guaranteed.

- It has a guaranteed 4 plus percent tax deferred rate of return.

- You never have to worry about what the stock market is doing.

- When you die, the death benefit goes 100% tax-free to your heirs.

- You have access to the cash value in the policy without penalties or restrictions.

- You reversed the flow of interest you are paying to the bank back to paying the interest to yourself.

- You pay no income and capital gains taxes on policy loans and most withdrawals.

- It does not require any dramatic life style changes and provides money for purchases and retirement needs.

- It helps you automatically pay off debt, invest and save at the same time.

- The interest and dividends are paid on all the money you have put into the policy even if you have borrowed money from the policy to spend.

- There are no restrictions like you find in qualified retirement plans and you can have larger contributions than most traditional qualified plans. Also, the limits have nothing to do with your income. Investment growth is tax-deferred, withdrawals are tax-free and inheritance income is tax-free.

- You have unrestricted liquidity, control and use of your money for any reason.

- In many states these assets are protected from creditors, judgments and lawsuits.

- You can build your wealth tax-free.

- Withdraw your wealth tax-free.

- Pay off your cars, home, student loans, credit cards while simultaneously building retirement wealth using the same dollars.

To learn more about the Private Family Bank read John Cummuta's 2017 book *The Banker's Secret to Permanent Family Wealth: Live your life . . . And build your wealth . . . Using the same money.* Most insurance salesman are unaware of this type of policy so for more information on the Private Family Bank designed for dentist contact: https://smartestwealthsystems.com/PFB-for-dentists

OPTION 2: CONSERVATIVE, LOW-RISK, LOW-RETURN INVESTMENTS

If you are risk-averse, cannot take a 10% to 20% drop in the market, and you need your money to live on in the next five to seven years, then you should invest more in CDs, bonds, and US treasuries. Do not put this money in bond mutual funds or ETFs because of their recent low returns and rising interest rates. The following three strategies are your better options.

Option 2a: Schwab money market account (SWVXX) is a good interim place for your money while you are waiting to buy index funds. As of this writing, their 7-day yield is about 2.3%. These are not FDIC insured but they are SIPC insured up to $500,000. This fund is available for individual retirement and investment accounts. If your account is a corporation or trust or 401(k), then you would either use the Schwab Government Money Fund (SWVXX) or the Schwab Treasury Obligations Money Fund (SNOXX), both returning about 2%.

Option 2b—Short-term treasury bills or notes and FDIC-insured CDs. These investments are considered true safety for those who do not want to take any risk and need funds available within the next five to seven years. When this book was written in January 2019, the daily treasury yield curve rates for six months was around 2.4%, and for one year the rates were about 2.6%, which barely keeps up with inflation. You can buy these online through treasurydirect.gov or through Charles Schwab and pay no commission. If you choose to work with one of the Schwab brokers, the trade will be $25. If you worry about fluctuations in the stock market, this is a good place to put your money. A Treasury Bill (T-Bill) is a short-term debt obligation backed by the Treasury Department of the US government, which matures in less than one year. Other Treasury notes have maturities from two to ten years, while Treasury bonds have maturities of greater than ten years. These both pay interest semi-annually, and the only real difference between Treasury notes and bonds is their maturity length. The reason I recommend treasuries over bond exchange traded funds ETF's is because treasury bills are guaranteed. In 2018 the return for a one-year treasury was over 2% while the US bond fund was a -0.03%.

OPTION 3: MEDIUM TO HIGH RISK, MEDIUM TO HIGH RETURN

Option 3a: Schwab and Vanguard target date index retirement funds. These funds have the lowest expense ratios for target index retirement funds, ranging from 0.08% to 0.16%. What makes target date funds different from other mutual funds is asset rebalancing based on your target date for retirement. That is, the fund adjusts for you over time; it helps you avoid making snap decisions that can affect a savings plan, like buying when markets are rising or selling when they fall. Compared to competitive products, target date funds seek more opportunity for growth in the early years, and then gradually place an increasing emphasis on stability up to retirement and beyond. Dr. Doug Carlsen, the dentist and national investment author, consultant and advisor has 90% of his personal investments in target date funds.

In the years before your retirement, a higher proportion of your assets are invested in equities to provide more growth potential and the opportunity to build your assets and keep up with inflation. The specific allocation changes, depending on how far away you are from your target retirement date. As you get close to retirement, the investment mix changes, with a higher proportion of your assets invested in bonds and cash investments to seek the increased stability and income you will need in retirement. After retirement, when your target date is reached, the assets in your fund continue to be invested more conservatively. The bond allocation increases, and the stock exposure decreases to help protect your investment, while still providing some opportunity for growth.

One example is the Vanguard Target Retirement 2045 Fund (ticker symbol VTTSX), with around 90% of investments in US and international stocks, and around 10 % in US and international bond funds. The expense ratio is 0.15%, and the ten-year return has been 10.3%, while over the same time frame, the S&P 500 index fund returned **13%**. Someone who's coming close to retirement may select the Vanguard Target Retirement 2015 Fund (ticker symbol VTXVX), with 43% in US and international total stock funds and 57% in US and international bond funds, with an expense ratio of 0.13% and a ten-year return of 8.1%. (See the chart below.) Also note that this bond-heavy fund did drop considerably in 2008, the worst recent year, by a -24.1% compared to the S&P 500 that dropped -36.7%. During the best year, 2013, the S&P 500 was up 32.3% compared to the lowest-risk bond fund which only did 13%. To check out the performance of any stock or mutual fund, go to Finance.yahoo.com, type in the ticker symbol and hit the performance bar. This is where the information in these charts were found.

Schwab and Vanguard Retirement Target Fund Return Comparison 1/1/2019 (Morningstar.com)									
	Schwab S&P 500 index fund	Vanguard target 2060 fund	Vanguard target 2045 fund	Vanguard target 2025 fund	Vanguard target 2015 fund	Schwab target 2060 fund	Schwab target 2045 fund	Schwab target 2025 fund	Schwab target 2015 fund
Ticker	SWPPX	VTTSX	VTIVX	VTTVX	VTXVX	SWYNX	SWYHX	SWYDX	SWYBX
Expense	0.03%	0.16%	0.16%	0.14%	0.14%	0.08%	0.08%	0.08%	0.08%
Cost/ 1M$	$300	$1600	$1600	$1400	$1400	$800	$800	$800	$800
Stocks	100%	87.51%	87.60%	62.9%	43.21%	92.9%	86.28%	58.95%	38.15%
Bonds		9.70%	9.70%	34.20%	53.53%	4.22%	9.37%	32.32%	50.93%
Cash		1.59%	1.51%	1.79%	2.61%	1.13%	2.72%	7.53%	10.07%
Other		1.19%	1.19%	1.11%	0.94%	1.75%	1.63%	1.19%	0.84%
Best 2013	32.3%	24.35%	24.37%	18.14%	13.00%				
Worst 2008	-36.7%		-34.56%	-30.05%	-24.06%				
Inception	5/19/1997	1/19/2012	10/27/2003	10/27/2003	10/27/2003	8/25/2016	8/25/2016	8/25/2016	8/25/2016
1 year	-4.4%	-7.9%	-7.9%	-5.6%	-3.3%	-8.0%	-7.3%	-4.3%	-2.1%
3 years	9.2%	6.8%	6.8%	9.7%	4.5%				
5 years	8.4%	5.1%	5.1%	5.4%	4.0%				
10 year	13.0%		10.3%	9.3%	8.1%				
15 year	7.8%		6.5%	6.15%	5.42%				

Option 3b: **Vanguard Life Strategy funds.** These are a series of broadly diversified, low-cost funds with an all-index, fixed allocation approach that may provide a complete portfolio in a single fund. They have an expense ratio of 0.11% to 0.14%. The four funds, each with a different allocation, target various risk-based objectives. These divide investments over three fund classes: total stock market index fund, total international stock index fund, and total US bond index fund. They rebalance each year. If you have a longer time horizon before you need the money and are willing to take a little more risk, then you may select the Vanguard LifeStrategy Growth Fund (ticker symbol VASGX), which holds 78% stocks and 22% bonds. Its ten-year return has been about 9.8% compared to the **13.1%** return of the S&P 500 fund. The next most conservative option is Vanguard LifeStrategy Moderate Growth Fund (ticker symbol VSMGX), with 59% stocks and 41% bonds. Its ten-year return has been about 8.4%. If you are much more conservative, then you would choose the Vanguard

LifeStrategy conservative growth fund (ticker symbol VSCGX), which holds around 40% in stocks and 60 % in bonds. Its ten-year return has been about 6.9%. The Income Fund (ticker symbol VASIX) is the most conservative and seeks to provide current income and some capital appreciation. The fund holds 80% of its assets in bonds, a portion of which are allocated to international bonds, and 20% in stocks, a portion of which are allocated to international stocks. Its ten-year return has been about 5.3%. Also note that the 40/60 bond-heavy fund did drop considerably in 2008, the worst year, by a -19.52%, compared to the S&P 500 that dropped -36.7%. In the best year, 2013, the S&P 500 was up 32.3% compared to the low risk 40/60 bond fund which only did 3.4%. To check out the performance of any stock or mutual fund, go to Finance.yahoo.com, type in the ticker symbol and hit the performance bar to check where these charts were found.

Vanguard Life Strategy Funds returns 1/1/2019 (Morningstar.com)					
	Vanguard S&P500 Index	Vanguard life strategy growth fund	Vanguard life strategy moderate growth fund	Vanguard life strategy conservative growth fund	Vanguard life strategy income fund
Ticker	VFIAX	VASGX	VSMGX	VSCGX	VASIX
Expense	0.04%	0.14%	0.13%	0.12%	0.11%
Stock/Bond ratio	100/0	80/20	60/40	40/60	20/80
US Stocks	100%	48.3%	36.4%	24.3%	12.1%
International Stocks		32%	23.9%	15.9%	7.9%
US Bonds		13.8%	27.9%	41.9%	56.1%
International Bonds		5.9%	11.8%	17.9%	23.9%
Best 2013	32.3%	21.2%	15.04%	9.08%	3.40%
Worst 2008	-36.7%	-34.39%	-26.5%	-19.52%	-10.53%
Inception	5/19/1997	9/30/1994	9/30/1994	9/30/1994	9/30/1994
1 Year	-4.3%	-6.9%	-4.9%	-3.3%	-1.1%
3 year	9.2%	6.3%	5.3%	4.2%	3.5%
5 year	8.5%	5.0%	4.5%	4.0%	3.4%
10 year	13.1%	9.5%	8.2%	6.9%	5.2%

OPTION 4: HIGH RISK—HIGH RETURN.

Buy the S&P 500 or the total US stock market index mutual funds or ETFs. To me, these are considered the gold standard for index funds, as they perform better than 96% of all other actively managed mutual funds. Warren Buffett has said that before he dies, he will put the inheritance for his children into a Vanguard S&P 500 fund and recommend they do not touch it.

Both Vanguard and Schwab have both S&P 500 index mutual funds and ETFs. You can buy the Schwab S&P 500 index mutual fund (ticker symbol SWPPX) at the expense ratio of 0.03%, or the Vanguard 500 index mutual fund (ticker symbol VFIAX) with an expense ratio of 0.04%, both providing an average annual return over a ten-year period of about 13.1%. Or you can buy Schwab US Broad Total Market index mutual fund (ticker symbol SWTSX) at the expense ratio of 0.03%, or the Vanguard Total Stock Market Index ETF (ticker symbol VTI) with an expense ratio of 0.04%, both returning an average annual return over a ten-year period of 13%.

Comparing average annual returns for Schwab and Vanguard Index funds 1/1/2019 (Morningstar.com)								
	S&P 500 Index				Total US Stock Market Index			
	Vanguard S&P 500 MF	Vanguard S&P 500 ETF	Schwab S&P 500 MF	Schwab S&P 500 like ETF	Schwab Total US Stock MF	Schwab Total US Stock ETF	Vanguard Total US Stock MF	Vanguard Total US Stock ETF
Ticker symbol	VFIAX	VOO	SWPPX	SCHX	SWTSX	SCHB	VTSAX	VTI
Expense ratio	0.04%	0.04%	0.03%	0.03%	0.03%	0.03%	0.04%	0.04%
# of stocks	509	509	509	771	2728	2432	3680	3680
Distribution	4.75	4.73	1.66	1.79	1.53	1.77	1.26	2.6
1 year	-4.3%	-4.5%	-4.4%	-4.5%	-5.3%	-5.3%	-5.2%	-5.2%
3 years	9.2%	9.3%	9.2%	9.2%	8.9%	8.9%	9.0%	9.0%
5 years	8.5%	8.5%	8.4%	8.3%	7.8%	7.9%	7.9%	7.9%
10 years	13.1%		13.0%		13.2%		13.3%	13.3%
15 Years	7.8%		7.7%		8.0%		8.0%	8.1%

In 2017, I attended Berkshire Hathaway's annual meeting in Omaha, Nebraska. I sat about 70 feet from Warren Buffett when he was talking about the bet he made with one of the large hedge fund managers. In 2007, Warren Buffett entered a bet for $1 million to be given to charity with the fund manager of Protégé Partners; he bet that the S&P 500 would beat a basket of hedge funds over the next decade. Warren Buffett looked out at the large crowd of 40,000 attendees and divided us in half. He said to those of us on the right side of the room that we were just average investors who could only afford to put our money in an index fund such as the S&P 500 and would settle for whatever it produced. But the 20,000 attendees on the left had a lot of available money; some were millionaires and could afford to pay 4.3% of their assets in fees to a hedge fund manager and 3% to hedge fund brokers each year to get extremely high returns. The fees paid to these hedge funds would average $98 billion a year.

Ten years after that bet, in 2017, the S&P 500 index fund had compounded an annual gain of 8.5% over the ten years, beating the average increase of 2.4% earned by the basket of funds selected by Protégé Partners. This is another example of keeping it simple and staying away from high fees.

You should not invest in the market the money you need to live on for the next five years. The Schwab money market account (SWVXX) is a good vehicle to place the money you need for the next five years, but you still can invest in the S&P 500 or total US market, buying index funds with your excess monies. Here are some criteria to help you decide. **You can invest mostly into stock index funds if**:

- You do not need the money for five years.
- You are working and have a higher income and savings related to your living expenses.
- You have no debt and a high net worth.
- You have greater investment knowledge and higher

risk tolerance, knowing when the market drops, that is time to buy, not sell.

- You are retired, debt-free and have enough income coming in from your Social Security, pension, dividends and working part-time to meet your financial needs.

- You have maximized your Private Family Bank to safely store some of your money in a tax-deferred environment that has a guaranteed rate of return.

REMEMBER TO STOP THE NOISE

I recommend that you only start investing when you are completely debt-free, because paying off debt gives you the highest rate of return without risk or fees. As you create a retire-in-practice model, you will find all the abundance that you need and will never think about so-called retirement. Continue to invest each month in your Private Family Bank and add to your stock portfolio when you see greater than 15% drop in the market—this is the best time to buy. And never get out of the market during these drops. And never get out of the market. A YouTube clip from the classic television series *Bob Newhart,* "Stop it," reminds us to stop our negative self-talk, worries and anxieties over investing and what's happening in the market. Stop listening to the financial news and focus on living and enjoying life. If you want true peace, stop listening to all the news. Once you have implemented *Dr. Ace's Financial Freedom Guide*, you can focus your energies on what you love, including the people in your life.

ABOUT THE AUTHOR

Dr. Ace Goerig graduated from Case Western Reserve University Dental School in 1971 and was their distinguished alumnus in 2014. He then joined the US Army and retired as a colonel in 1991 after 20 years. He is a diplomat of the American Board of Endodontists and has been in private practice for 28 years in Olympia, Washington. Dr. Goerig has presented at every major national dental meeting and in 1996, co-founded Endo Mastery, a coaching program for endodontists.

In 2004, Dr. Goerig coauthored *Time and Money: Your Guide to Economic Freedom* with Kendrick Mercer to teach doctors and team members the secrets of becoming personally and financially free.

Dr. Ace has established two free websites to help dentists and their teams become financially free. They are DoctorAce.com and DebtFreeDentist.com. He and his wife, Nancy, were married in 1969 and have five children and 13 grandchildren.

www.ingramcontent.com/pod-product-compliance
Lightning Source LLC
Chambersburg PA
CBHW021432180326
41458CB00001B/231